THE TANK MUSEUM IN 100 OBJECTS

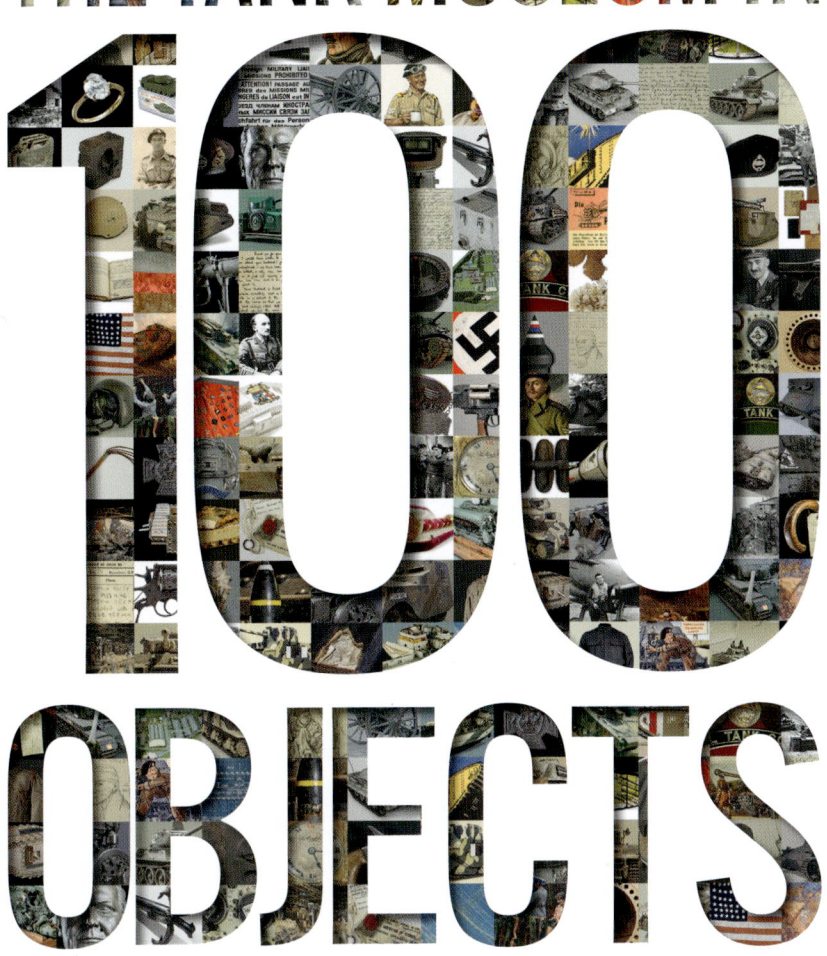

DAVID WILLEY

CONTENTS

INTRODUCTION P4

#001 P6
THE FIRST EVER TANK SHELL TO BE FIRED

#002 P8
ROSE HENRIQUES' RING

#003 P10
THE GOC
ERIC KENNINGTON RA

#004 P12
TEST PLATE

#005 P14
SPLINTER MASK

#006 P16
FIELD MARSHAL CARVER'S BATON

#007 P18
VICKERS 6-TON TANK

#008 P20
RICARDO TANK ENGINE

#009 P22
'JERRY' CAN

#010 P24
MARK 7 COMBAT HELMET WITH BULLET DAMAGE

#011 P26
CAPTAIN RICHARD WAIN'S VICTORIA CROSS

#012 P28
BOILING VESSEL

#013 P30
BONE DOME

#014 P32
THE TANK, SIR FRANK BRANGWYN RA

#015 P34
LITTLE AUDREY ABBESS OF CHANTRY

#016 P36
THE BOOK OF COMMON PRAYER

#017 P38
MONTY'S BERET

#018 P40
'LITTLE WILLIE' THE FIRST TANK

#019 P42
FLAGS OF FREEDOM

#020 P44
P6 COMPASS

#021 P46
DAMAGED BUST OF HERMANN GÖRING

#022 P48
THE BELSEN WHIP

#023 P50
GOLD-PLATED TANK

#024 P52
LANCE CORPORAL CHARLES NYE'S SINGLE-SHOT PISTOL

#025 P54
SIGHT FROM MAUS

#026 P56
MARK I TANK

#027 P58
DINKY No 651 CENTURION TANK

#028 P60
TANK CAMOUFLAGE MODEL PERCYVAL TUDOR-HART

#029 P62
ROLLS-ROYCE 1920 PATTERN ARMOURED CAR

#030 P64
VICKERS MEDIUM MARK II

#031 P66
CORPORAL STEPHEN KENNEDY MM MALCOLM McGREGOR

#032 P68
TIGER 131

#033 P70
CARRIERS IN PRODUCTION AT THE FORD MOTOR CO HELEN McKIE

#034 P72
BESA MACHINE-GUN

#035 P74
SEALED PATTERN WASHER

#036 P76
TANK SUIT

#037 P78
BLUEPRINT TRACING

#038 P80
PIAT PROJECTOR, INFANTRY, ANTI-TANK

#039 P82
LETTER HOME NORMAN AGER

#040 P84
MY SON JOHN LEONARD JOHN FULLER ROI, RCA

#041 P86
SCALE MODEL OF THE RARDE SITE AT CHERTSEY

#042 P88
THE COST

#043 P90
LIBERTY ENGINE

#044 P92
SHERMAN V

#045 P94
BLOWN 2-POUNDER BARREL

#046 P96
PANZERFAUST

#047 P98
RAM KANGAROO

#048 P100
TOG II*

#049 P102
BRIXMIS SOUVENIR SIGN

#050 P104
SHERMAN TANK 'MICHAEL'

#051 P106
STUART HAMILTON'S PHOTO ALBUM

© The Tank Museum 2023
All rights reserved. No part of this publication may be reproduced or stored in a retrieval system or transmitted, in any form or by any means, electronic, mechanical, photocopying, recording or otherwise, without prior permission in writing from The Tank Museum.
Designed and produced for The Tank Museum by JJN Publishing Ltd.
Production Director: Nigel Clements
Editorial Director: Jonathan Falconer
Art Director: Jud Webb
Photography: Matt Sampson, Alastair Jennings
Pre-press: Gary Stuckey
Thanks to: Olivia Coughlan, Theodore Gurney, Ian Hudson, Laura Sweetenham, Marjolijn Verbrugge.
First published in 2023 by The Tank Museum.
David Willey has asserted his moral right to be identified as the author of this work.
British Library Cataloguing in Publication Data.
A catalogue record for this book is available from the British Library.
Printed book ISBN 978-1-7399027-8-0
Printed and bound in Malta.

#052 P108
A TANK IN ACTION

#053 P110
MARK V

#054 P112
FIRST MESSAGE TO A TANK IN ACTION

#055 P114
ARMOURED BARREL MG 34

#056 P116
WARTIME SKETCHBOOK

#057 P118
CAMOUFLAGE NET

#058 P120
CRESTED CHINA TANK

#059 P122
THE 'FURY' TANK

#060 P124
TANK IN TOWN POSTER

#061 P126
CAMBRAI FLAG

#062 P128
THE GRAINCOURT GUN

#063 P130
CAPTURED SWASTIKA FLAG

#064 P132
WEBLEY MARK VI REVOLVER

#065 P134
DILLON'S WALKING STICK

#066 P136
THE RPG-7

#067 P138
17-POUNDER DISCARDING SABOT AMMUNITION

#068 P140
MODEL OF HM LCT 7051

#069 P142
ACTION MAN SCORPION TANK

#070 P144
STANDARD BEAVERETTE

#071 P146
NEEDLEWORK BADGE

#072 P148
DIARIES AND LETTERS

#073 P150
STURMMÖRSERWAGEN 606/4 MIT 38CM RW 61

#074 P152
ROYAL TANK CORPS UNIFORM (1935)

#075 P154
PANZERBEFEHLSWAGEN GERMAN COMMAND TANK

#076 P156
M3 GRANT TANK

#077 P158
ROLLS-ROYCE METEOR ENGINE

#078 P160
J.F.C. FULLER'S ALBUM

#079 P162
T34/85

#080 P164
ORPEN'S LETTERS TO ELLIOTT HOTBLACK

#081 P166
THE BLACK BERET

#082 P168
MECHANISATION POSTCARD

#083 P170
QAIMNS NURSE'S CAPE

#084 P172
SWEETHEART BROOCH

#085 P174
MAUSER 1918 T-GEWEHR

#086 P176
ROYAL TANK CORPS LOCOMOTIVE NAMEPLATES

#087 P178
ESCAPE ROUTE 1940

#088 P180
WALTER RATCLIFFE'S UNIFORM

#089 P182
CLEMENT ARNOLD'S WATCH

#090 P184
SCRATCH-BUILT 1/12TH SCALE KING TIGER

#091 P186
AIR OBSERVATION CARDS OF THE FIRST TANK ATTACK

#092 P188
MARTEL TANK MASCOT

#093 P190
CENTURION

#094 P192
T-54 TANK

#095 P194
VICKERS TANK PERISCOPE MARK IV

#096 P196
GUN BARREL DISPLAY

#097 P198
STURMGESCHÜTZ

#098 P200
WIRELESS SET NO 19

#099 P202
JOHNSON 'SNAKE' TRACK

#100 P204
MARK I BLUEPRINT

INDEX P206

MUSEUM REFERENCE NUMBERS EXPLAINED

Every item in The Tank Museum collection, from the largest tank to the smallest badge, has its own unique entry number, or 'E' number. The aim is to ensure that every item can be quickly and unambiguously identified, and that it can be linked to related records such as details about the donor, any connected objects or documents, and any stories related to them.

E2017.2398.1

Using the example above, the first number after the 'E' is the year in which the object was acquired. The second number, after the full stop, is simply the next available number for acquisitions from that year. Some objects have a second full stop and a third number. This tells us it was acquired as part of a larger collection, for example one of a group of medals.

INTRODUCTION

The Tank Museum houses the historic collections of the Royal Armoured Corps and the Royal Tank Regiment. It has a collecting policy that is broadly interpreted as 'telling the story of tanks and those who served in them'. In the collection of over 100,000 catalogued items it has vehicles, uniforms, medals, works of art, models, documents, insignia, photographs, weapons, toys and memorabilia.

So, what makes it into a list of 100 great objects as opposed to any other item in The Tank Museum's extensive collections? I will cut straight to the point – I chose it. As with any collection, they, the items, can be approached in so many ways; the subjective personal favourite, a significance in the technical story, the outstanding skill or craftsmanship shown, the special rarity or the emotional engagement. One thing is certain, though: the list of how one might choose 'great' objects could go on indefinitely.

I have used the above and other criteria to select these 100 items. Someone else might come up with 100 different objects and make as good a book, or even a better one. But now, having been the Curator at The Tank Museum for over 20 years, it falls to me to choose and write a little on each item.

I hope this selection gives a range of the museum's holdings, not simply the vehicles that will take primacy in the minds of most people. I have tried to avoid writing just a catalogue entry; if you wish to know an engine size or technical specification of a vehicle, there are now so many websites, books and apps that can give you that information in a moment. Here, I have looked for a story, a significance about an item, although inevitably facts and figures do feature.

The Tank Museum, like most other museums, is still collecting. I hope that this volume might inspire more items to be discovered and stories written up to be added to our collection, and in turn, benefit the wider public. Alas, some of the most recent military operations of the Royal Armoured Corps are perhaps the least represented. Although they might at the time be the most recorded with digital imagery and text, they are the least 'saved' with hard drives being wiped, lost or not backed up and access limited. The digital era will bring new challenges on collecting. Of one thing I have no doubt: that the undefinable but magical appeal of the 'real thing' will continue to bring visitors to The Tank Museum. I hope you will enjoy discovering some of that magic surrounding these historic items and their stories from the collection, showcased in the pages of this book.

David Willey, Curator
2023

#001 E1968.76.2
THE FIRST EVER TANK SHELL TO BE FIRED

The first shell to be fired from the first tank on 20 January 1916 was the result of a misfire and needed to be retrieved with a spade.

The first trials of 'Mother' at Burton Park near Lincoln were supposed to be secret, but it appears to have had a social dimension as wives and guests are also present.

The first prototype rhomboid-shaped tank ended up with a number of names: 'Mother' is perhaps best-known, 'Big Willie' less so, and the official nameplate affixed to the tank was HMLS *Centipede*. Fosters of Lincoln completed the vehicle in late November 1915. The weapons to be carried were only decided upon at a late stage in the design process.

A 2.95in mountain gun was borrowed from Woolwich Arsenal and was considered good, but an appropriate supply was not available.

The Admiralty – heavily involved in the construction and testing of the new vehicles – suggested 6-pounder (pdr) guns, spares of which were available from naval stocks. Called a 6pdr because the solid shot fired by the gun weighed 6lb (2.7kg) in the Imperial measurement system, this is a way of describing gun size that dates back to Napoleonic times.

To test the effect on the hull of a gun firing from a sponson – the bay window structure on the side of the hull – 'Mother' was taken to a field near Lincoln. An armour-piercing, solid round was brought up from London by Major Hetherington from the Royal Naval Air Service accompanied by Albert Stern, a banker who would be put in charge of tank production. Hetherington fired the gun but nothing happened; a misfire. As the gun was examined from inside 'Mother', the weapon went off but no one was tracing the fall of shot. Albert Stern later wrote, 'No one knew where the shell had gone. We feared the worst. Lincoln Cathedral was in danger!' However, Stern went on, '... after two hours spent with a spade the shell was found buried in the earth, to the great relief of us all.'

The shell was later presented to Lady Tritton, wife of the Fosters director and tank designer Sir William Tritton. Mounted on a presentation stand, the projectile was presented to The Tank Museum by the Tritton family in 1968.

Glass from the viewing prism in Basil Henriques' Mark I tank shattered in his face as he was looking through it. One of the fragments was made into a ring for his new wife, Rose. She wore it for many years before donating it to The Tank Museum in the 1960s.

#002 E1963.3

ROSE HENRIQUES' RING

A piece of shattered glass that had embedded itself in Basil Henriques' face at the Battle of Flers-Courcelette was removed by doctors and made into a ring for his wife.

Basil Henriques was an unlikely figure to command a tank during the very first tank attack on 15 September 1916. The son of wealthy Jewish parents, he was educated at Harrow then Oxford. He began his life-long work with young people by setting up a Jewish Boys Club in the East End of London in 1913. Henriques described himself as tall, ungainly and not particularly good soldier material. His wife Rose said of him: 'For a more unlikely candidate for military prowess can seldom have presented himself before a Commanding Officer.'

However, he was granted a commission and found himself attending an interview with his new-found friend George Macpherson about a new secret role. Both were accepted as the 'right sort', but were unaware of what exactly they had volunteered for.

At the Battle of Flers-Courcelette, 26-year-old Lieutenant Basil Henriques was in command of a Mark I tank. As the tank progressed towards enemy positions it came under heavy artillery fire. One accurate blast smashed the thick glass vision prism that Henriques was looking through to direct his vehicle, embedding shards and splinters in his face. He later recalled: 'A smash against my flap in front caused splinters to come in and the blood to pour down my face. Then our prism glass broke to pieces, then another smash, I think it must have been a bomb right in my face.'

Basil and Rose on their wedding day in 1916. Rose was the recipient of Basil's letters and became the family archivist, creating albums of press cuttings, letters and photographs.

His wife Rose received the news of his injury in a telegram which read: 'Regret to inform you that 2Lt. Henriques, Machine Gun Corps admitted to Red Cross hospital, Rouen Sept 17th with gunshot wound face slight. Further news send when received. Secretary War Office.'

Henriques was fortunate to escape more serious injury and the glass splinters were removed from his face by medics. One piece was large enough to be mounted as a 'stone' in a gold ring, which he gave to his wife as a memento of his brush with danger.

Henriques returned to France after convalescence to serve as a Reconnaissance Officer with the tanks and survived the war. He dedicated the rest of his life to social work, and particularly the social welfare of children. He was knighted in 1955 and a road in Whitechapel in London's East End is named after him. His wife, Rose, donated the ring to The Tank Museum in the 1960s along with an album recording his wartime activities.

Kennington has captured so well the steely look of concentration on Hobart's face. He also completed another portrait of the general standing at a lectern, which is also in The Tank Museum collection.

#003 E1979.16

THE GOC
ERIC KENNINGTON RA (1888–1960)

An Official War Artist in both world wars, Kennington was also a gifted sculptor best known for his 24th Division War Memorial in London's Battersea Park.

Eric Kennington served in the infantry in the First World War, and was invalided out of the Army in June 1915. He was appointed an official War Artist in 1917 and returned to France to mainly draw portraits – his skills as a draughtsman were already widely admired. He worked with his friend and hero T.E. Lawrence to illustrate Lawrence's book *The Seven Pillars of Wisdom*. Kennington undertook a number of sculptural commissions in the interwar period, including carving an effigy of Lawrence in St Martin's Church at Wareham in Dorset.

Kennington was approached by the War Artist Advisory Committee in November 1939 and began a series of commissions to portray those contributing to the war effort. These included famous figures and those who performed heroic acts in the defence of their country. As a reviewer aptly described, 'his technique has a force admirably suited to conveying unflinching and dauntless resolution ... and evoke palpably in a portrait ... the savour and essence of courage.' They are some of the most evocative and greatest works of art of the war.

In December 1941, Kennington travelled to Yorkshire to visit the snowbound camp of the 11th Armoured Division where he completed a series of portraits that would be published in *Tanks and Tank Folk*. His host, Major Humphrey Moore of the Westminster Dragoons wrote, 'He does not really draw – he sculpts in chalks'.

Kennington had known Percy Hobart, the subject of the pastel portrait, since 1919. The Commander of the 11th Armoured Division was 'a leader in rapid mechanised warfare. These qualities are to think, act with decision and give orders at speed and clearly.' Moore continued, 'Kennington has captured him and his character in an hour with half-a-dozen-pieces of chalk.' The pastel portrait shows Hobart in a tank turret, wrapped up against the bitter weather with map case in hand.

Hobart was a distinctive, and to some, abrasive, character. After being sacked in 1940, he joined the Home Guard as a corporal. Churchill reinstated Hobart in 1941, leading to his promotion from corporal to major general.

This page: the inner face of a piece of armour-testing plate showing penetration by the tip of a 17pdr armour-piercing (AP) round.

Opposite: the outer face, showing the protruding base of the projectile with a hole in its centre for the tracer element.

#004 E2023.136
TEST PLATE

When armour plate is penetrated by a high velocity round, the kinetic energy it produces creates lethal metal fragments that fly around inside the tank wounding or killing the crew.

Traditionally three factors make up a tank: firepower, mobility and protection. Vehicles are always a compromise between these key features. Here we can see a projectile (the firepower) and some armour plate (the protection).

The most obvious and probable type of attack on a tank dictates the level and area of armour protection. For tanks, the thickest armour is usually placed on the front as this is the most likely direction of incoming fire. Placing the same thickness of armour all around a tank will likely create a vehicle that is too heavy and, in turn, less mobile.

Britain's first tanks had 14mm (½in) face-hardened armour plate, which could stop bullets but little else. It could buckle when it was made and was unmachinable after the hardening process. Rolled homogenous armour (RHA) plate could be machined, and if it was an appropriate thickness, it could stop the kinetic energy of high velocity rounds. Kinetic energy is the power given to the projectile by its motion, which is created by the propellant as it is fired from a gun. The more kinetic energy, the more armour plate that is needed to defeat it.

Cast armour was used on tanks such as the Renault FT in the First World War. Castings have to be about 10 per cent thicker than rolled homogenous armour to create the same level of protection, because the metal has a coarser grain structure.

The British measurement system used to describe gun size was a very old one dating back to Napoleonic times. It refers to the weight of the solid projectile fired by the gun – 17 pounds (lb) in Imperial weight. In 1941, Britain started designing the 17-pounder (pdr) gun as a replacement for the earlier 2- and 6pdr pieces. It was a very successful weapon that was fitted to the Challenger A30 and Sherman Firefly tanks, as well as the Achilles and Archer tank destroyers. This was considered adequate at the time, but before the war's end a 20 and 32lb round had also been developed.

This piece of armour-testing plate (measuring 115mm or 4½in thick) has been fired at by a 17pdr gun. The armour-piercing projectile, made of steel, has penetrated but become stuck in the armour plate. British armour-piercing projectiles carried a tracer element in the base so the flight could be tracked by the gunner. The solid projectile did not, however, have a bursting charge inside – unlike the German equivalent.

#005 E2013.2500

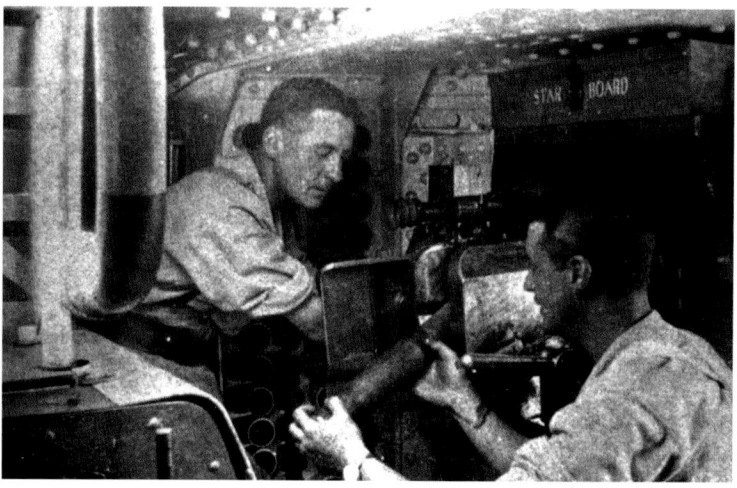

SPLINTER MASK

Face masks were issued to tank crewmen to protect against bullet splash, but in the heat and claustrophobia of the tank they were not popular.

Conditions in the first tanks were appalling for the crews. Vehicles had no suspension so the men were flung about when crossing rough ground, while engines created a stifling heat and exhaust manifolds leaked fumes into the cab. Machine-gun fire could cause bullet splash to enter the vehicle. The core of bullets was made of lead, a soft metal that on impact with an armour plate could fragment – or splash – and find its way into the tank through gaps in the riveted armour or vision ports. Paint and metal on the inside of the vehicle was also seen to flake off when bullets impacted exterior metal surfaces, a phenomenon known as 'spalling'.

To try and help protect the eyes of the crew, face or 'splinter' masks were issued. Driver Arthur Jenkin described the mask as 'a steel padded in leather, the eyes protected by small flat steel bars 1/16th of an inch apart, and a steel chain about 6 inches by 3 inches hangs over the mouth and chin, very similar to the face armour worn by knights in the Middle Ages.'

The masks gave yet another de-humanising element to the new and frightening weapon that was the tank.

When issued, masks bore a small card label advising the wearer that, 'The curvature of this mask may be adjusted to your face by slightly bending'. Photographs show crews with the masks around their necks as if wearing a badge of office, and masks often seem to have been saved as mementos of service. In consequence, The Tank Museum has been donated quite a number of saved and treasured splinter masks over the years.

Original splinter masks were made from metal covered with thick leather. They featured slatted eye pieces and a chain mail 'apron' suspended from metal ring fasteners to cover the mouth.

Opposite:
Gunner and loader of a 'Male' tank at their stations. The engine is to their left and when running drowned out conversation.

THE TANK MUSEUM IN 100 OBJECTS

#006 E2003.1441.1

FIELD MARSHAL CARVER'S BATON

As a symbol of power and high office, the gold-tipped baton was awarded on appointment to the rank of Field Marshal.

The metal baton is covered in scarlet velvet on which are fixed gilt heraldic lions. On its gold top is a mounted figure of St George, also in gold, slaying the dragon. The base (left) is in gold and bears the inscription: 'From Her Majesty Queen Elizabeth II, To Field-Marshal Sir Richard Michael Power Carver G.C.B., C.B.E., D.S.O., M.C 1973'. The baton is contained in a fitted scarlet velvet-covered case.

A portrait of Field Marshal Lord Carver commissioned by the Royal Tank Regiment and painted by Michael Noakes (1933–2018).

The Field Marshal's baton looks more like something out of a Harry Potter film than an ancient symbol of high military office. The idiom 'every soldier has the baton of a Field Marshal in his knapsack' may indicate the aspiration of the common soldier to reach the loftiest heights of command, but few would actually achieve this rank. In many ways, Michael Carver was an untypical example of one who did.

Michael Carver was born in 1915 and became a second lieutenant in the Royal Tank Corps in 1935. He was to rise to the highest position in the British military hierarchy, Chief of the Defence Staff, and was promoted to Field Marshal in July 1973.

Carver served in North Africa during the Second World War and was awarded the Military Cross. He was promoted and led the 1st Royal Tank Regiment, later becoming the 7th Armoured Brigade Commander in Normandy in June 1944 at the age of 29. His postwar career saw a further series of promotions and service in Kenya, the Far East and within NATO. Carver was not considered typical of high-ranking British officers – he was analytical and independent of thought, slashing the size of the Territorial Army in 1964 and arguing strongly against Britain's Trident nuclear programme.

Field Marshal is the highest rank in the British Army. Altogether 141 men have held the rank since 1736, with some lengthy periods where no Field Marshals were appointed. After the Second World War, an Army officer serving as Chief of the Defence Staff was promoted to Field Marshal on appointment – a practice that only stopped in the mid-1990s.

The rank insignia worn by a Field Marshal features two batons surrounded by yellow leaves under a crown. Awarded on appointment, the gold-tipped baton is carried by a Field Marshal at some ceremonial occasions. The baton as a symbol of power dates back to the mace – Egyptian pharaohs could be seen to carry a mace.

This baton is made by Garrards, the crown jewellers. It has an equestrian figure of St George slaying the dragon at one end and a personal inscription from the Queen at the other.

#007 E1952.28
VICKERS 6-TON TANK

As originator of the first tank and a leader in tank design, Vickers had an advantage in the lucrative overseas export market during the interwar years.

The Vickers '6-tonner' or 'E' for Export tank was a sales success in the 1930s and a major influence on tank design in many countries.

Vickers had originally made steel castings in Sheffield before moving into munitions, then merging with a similar manufacturer, Armstrong-Whitworth, in 1927. The War Office closed its Tank Design Department in 1923 and encouraged Vickers to continue with armoured vehicle design.

In the interwar years, mechanisation was discussed as a topic not just in military circles but also in the press: questions around how vehicles were going to replace the horse and how could, or should, tanks be used created enormous public interest. The British Army's Experimental Mechanised Force carried out exercises on Salisbury Plain in 1927 that were widely covered in the press. This led to many other countries wanting to experiment with armoured vehicles, especially tanks, in their own armies. Fortuitously, Vickers had a new 6-ton tank to offer for sale.

First built in 1928, the Type A model had two rotating turrets armed with Vickers .303in machine-guns; the Type B had a single turret with a 47mm gun and machine-gun in the same mount. The suspension system was patented by Vickers, comprising two axles that crossed the tank's hull and held a double bogie fitted with cantilever springs. Power was from a V8 air-cooled engine built by Armstrong Siddeley that drove a front sprocket through a four-speed gearbox. The tracks would last around 3,000 miles – a considerable achievement at that time.

Though the British Army did not put the tank into service it was purchased by eight countries, including Bolivia, where they were used in the little-known Gran Chaco War against Paraguay in 1933. The Soviet Union was the initial buyer, taking 15 examples, with the first tank arriving in late 1930 and the last in 1932. Soviet engineers attended the Vickers factory to learn about their construction and a licence agreement was signed that led to the tank's manufacture in the Soviet Union. It was called the T-26 with different armament arrangements fitted. As a reliable vehicle it continued to be developed in Soviet service with over 12,000 built before production ended in 1941.

In Newcastle, 6-ton Export tanks are lined up outside the doors of the Vickers works. This location was a regular photographic backdrop for vehicles.

The Vickers 6-ton, or Type E (for Export), was perhaps the most successful British tank never used by the British Army. Around 150 were built from 1928, selling to eight countries.

#008 E1949.227
RICARDO TANK ENGINE

The original Daimler tank engine lacked the power that the terrain of the Western Front demanded, so the War Office put together a specification for a replacement and Harry Ricardo rose to the challenge.

Harry Ricardo was a Cambridge graduate and brilliant engineer who took a special interest in internal combustion engines. In 1917, Ricardo was asked to design an engine to replace the Daimler Foster 105hp example being used in the first British tanks. The Daimler was very smoky and underpowered for the job it was expected to do on the rough ground of the First World War battlefields. The War Office stipulated a daunting list of requirements for the new engine.

Harry Ricardo – a mechanical genius who rose to the challenge of building a new tank engine.

It would have to fit the same space as the Daimler engine, but be 50 per cent more powerful at 150hp; not stall at 45-degree angles; be able to run for 100 hours without major adjustments; not use high-tensile steel and alloys as these were earmarked for the aeroplane industry; and run on the lowest grade fuel. The higher grade fuels went to the Royal Flying Corps.

Ricardo rose to the challenge and designed an engine that was being produced at 100 units a week in April 1917. Over 8,000 were made and it became the first British-designed engine to be mass-produced. Some examples were used in France to act as generators powering workshops and for lighting hospitals.

Harry Ricardo received £30,000 in royalties for his engine, allowing him to buy some land in Sussex where he set up a factory, the Bridge Works at Old Shoreham. Ricardo was influential in many engine and fuel developments, which resulted in him receiving a knighthood in 1948. The company bearing his name is still based at Shoreham and remains committed to the ethos of its founder, to 'maximise efficiency and eliminate waste'.

#009 E2015.354

'JERRY' CAN

Imitation by the Allies of the ingenious German-designed 'Jerry' can was the sincerest form of flattery.

Fuel containers were needed as soon as combustion powered vehicles started using roads. In Britain these took the form of square 2-gallon cans with a brass screw-top, often stamped or stencilled with the supplier's name.

In Germany, the military put out a requirement for a new 20-litre fuel container and in 1937 Vinzenz Grünvogel of Müller Engineering designed what would become the famous 'Jerry' can, or the Wehrmacht-Einheitskanister.

Grünvogel's design – so common to us now – has many simple but ingenious features. The three-piece handle allows for one full or two empty cans to be carried in one hand, as well as enabling cans to be passed along human chains. Recessed seams meant there was less chance of them being damaged in transit and the square shape allowed the cans to be stacked. Indentations on the flat surface helped give the can rigidity. The flip-top sealing cap allowed swift filling and emptying, while the positioning of it and the hollow handles meant there was enough buoyancy for a full can to float in water. Cans were also used to carry other fluids – water-carrying cans were often painted with a white cross to stop any confusion.

When captured in North Africa the cans were re-used by British forces and well-liked. Their own fuel containers – aptly known as 'flimsies' – contained 4 gallons (18 litres) and were made of tin plate with crimped or soldered seams that were weak and easily cracked, causing leaks. Often transported in pairs in a wire-and-wood cage, it was common for British flimsies to lose a third of their fuel when using this method.

The success of the 'Jerry' can named after the Germans, or 'Jerries' to the British, meant it was reverse engineered in both Britain and America with some small differences. The can became a vital means of supply in the advance across Europe after D-Day – the US forces alone requested 1.2 million a month to replace losses. Cans were supposed to be recycled but were often dumped at the roadside, so the US military offered money to French schoolchildren to collect and return them.

This British tank crew are using 'flimsies' as stools and tables while they cook their meal, possibly a better use for the can than holding petrol.

As well as giving rigidity, the stamped indentation on the sides also allowed expansion of the contents in hot theatres of operations like the North African desert. The embossed legend on the side of this 1940-pattern Jerry can made by Nowack AG, translates as 'Fuel, 20 litres, Flammable'.

#010 E2011.434

MARK 7 COMBAT HELMET WITH BULLET DAMAGE

Worn in Afghanistan by Lance Corporal Craig Murfitt of the 2nd Royal Tank Regiment, the Mark 7 Combat Helmet is credited with saving his life.

The Mark 7 helmet's liner features a mesh top section and padded panels around the head. A three-point suspension system/chin strap starts at the back of the helmet and runs forward to two adjusting straps, one on either side. A leather chin cup is provided to hold the helmet in place.

On 20 December 2010, Lance Corporal Craig Murfitt of the 2nd Royal Tank Regiment was on patrol in Afghanistan in a Warthog all-terrain vehicle. Murfitt identified a member of the Taliban on a rooftop, armed and about to fire on his vehicle. The Taliban insurgent was using a 10-year-old child as a human shield. Fearing that he would hit the child, Murfitt refrained from firing and awaited developments, hoping that the child would be released.

'I started to observe the man through the scope of my rifle. This is when he pulled a long barrelled weapon from behind the wall on the roof and took aim over the child's right-hand shoulder.... His weapon was pointing directly at my position. I knew I could fire first with the rules of engagement we were on, and take the gunman down but I could not guarantee the child would be unharmed. I then made a decision to wait for him to shoot at me first with the hope that he would miss and the child would move for me to take a clear shot.'

The insurgent fired and hit Murfitt. 'Then there was a massive thud to the side of my head as if someone

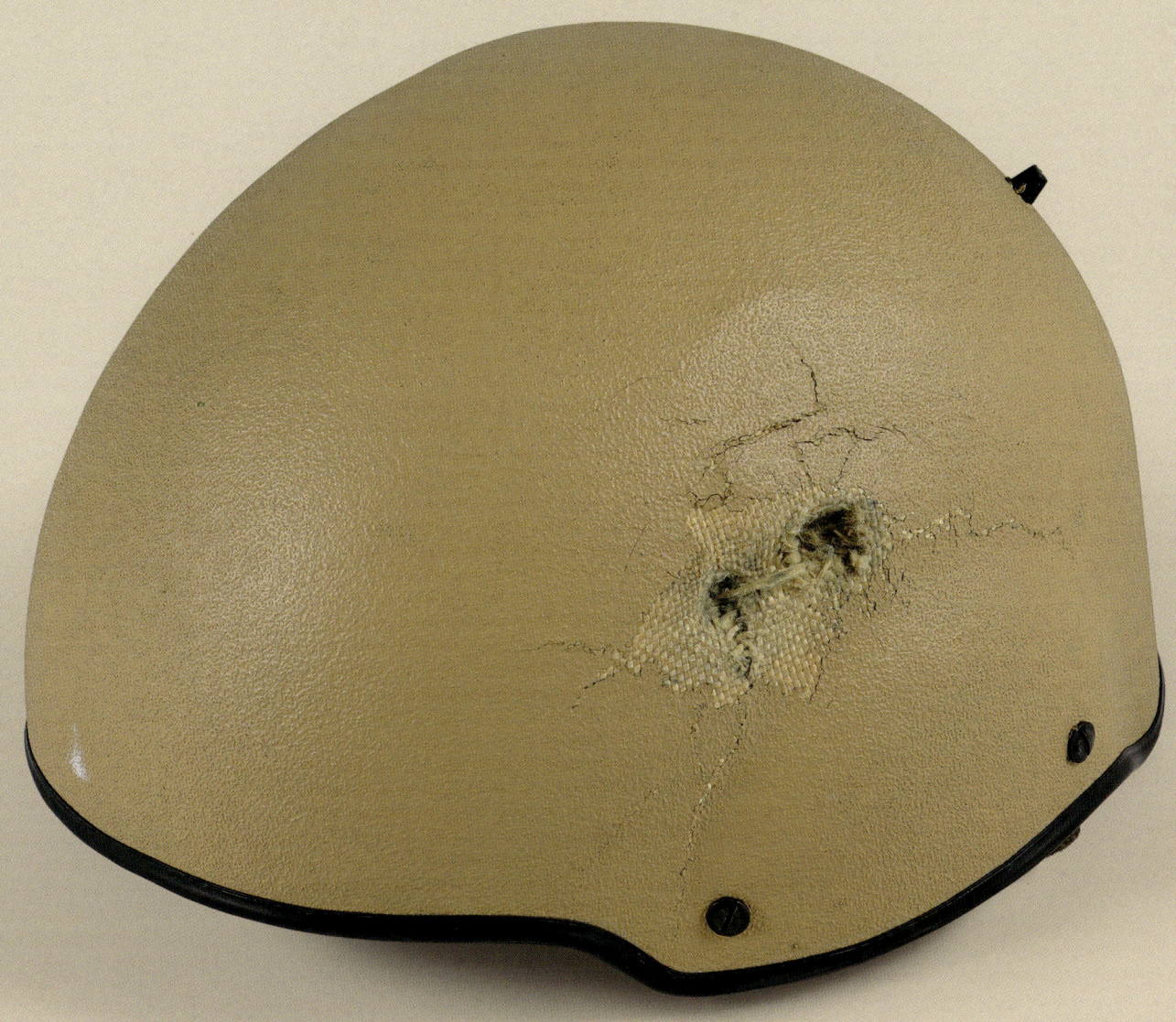

had hit the side of my helmet with a hammer. I fell to the floor seeing stars and my ears ringing.' Murfitt was able to report the situation to his commander who radioed other members of the patrol to engage the insurgent when the child had fled. Murfitt later wrote:

'I can honestly say that the decision I made that day was made easy knowing I had a great troop from a great regiment supporting everything I decided to do. I knew that their skills would get us out of whatever situation we were in. If I had to relive that situation again, I would not change the decision I made.'

It was found that the rifle fired by the Taliban was a vintage British .303in Lee Enfield. The Mark 7 Helmet helped absorb the impact of the round and was later inspected at the Defence Science and Technology Laboratory before Craig gave his helmet to The Tank Museum.

The Army recognises this type of behaviour as 'courageous restraint'. A soldier can sometimes be as brave and as effective by not firing at an enemy as they are by attacking them.

The metal jacket from the .303in round that hit Craig Murfitt.

Above: The helmet's ballistic nylon material prevented the insurgent's .303in round from penetrating the shell. Made by NP Aerospace Ltd, the Mark 7's shape allows a soldier to lie flat and shoot straight, without the rear rim digging into the body armour and tipping the front rim over their eyes.

#011 E2017.2398.1

CAPTAIN RICHARD WAIN'S VICTORIA CROSS

Richard Wain was 20 years old when he took part in the Battle of Cambrai and earned a posthumous Victoria Cross.

On 20 November 1917 at 6.10am, a major British assault on the town of Cambrai in north-west France began. The attack, involving over 400 tanks, was designed to push the German Army back and capture the strategically important town.

One of the many tank commanders in action that day was 20-year-old Richard Wain. He had joined the Tank Corps in early 1917, transferring from the Manchester Regiment. At Cambrai he was a captain and in charge of a section of Mark IV tanks. Shortly after 8.50am, Wain spotted a group of infantry soldiers who were pinned down by machine-gun fire. While trying to draw the fire away from these men, his tank *Abou-Ben-Adam II* was struck by mortar shells, killing six of the crew.

Captain Wain's subsequent actions led to a posthumous award of the Victoria Cross. His citation records:

'For most conspicuous bravery in command of a section of tanks. During the attack, his tank was disabled by a direct hit near an enemy strong point, which was holding up the attack. Captain Wain and one man, both seriously wounded, were the only survivors. Though bleeding profusely from his wounds, he refused the attention of stretcher bearers, rushed from behind the tank with a Lewis gun and captured the strong point, taking about half the garrison prisoners. Although his wounds were very serious, he picked up a rifle and continued to fire at the retiring enemy until he received a fatal wound in the head. It was due to the valour displayed by Captain Wain that the infantry were able to advance.'

Captain Richard Wain VC.

After the war, Richard Wain's parents Harris and Florence travelled from their home in Llandaff to Buckingham Palace to receive their son's Victoria Cross from King George V. Wain's selfless actions at the Battle of Cambrai are still remembered by the family today and they have loaned his Victoria Cross to The Tank Museum to 'share his memory with pride'.

Richard Wain was buried beside his wrecked tank but his grave was lost in the subsequent fighting. His name is among more than 7,000 commemorated on the Cambrai Memorial.

The Victoria Cross is Britain's highest award for gallantry. It was awarded to four members of the Tank Corps during the First World War – Richard Wain, Cecil Sewell, Clement Robertson and Richard West. Sadly, all four VCs were awarded posthumously. That which was won by Cecil Sewell is in The Tank Museum's permanent collection.

The cuboid-shaped Boiling Vessel is plugged into the vehicle's 24V electrical system. A junior member of a vehicle crew is often unofficially appointed as 'BV Commander' with responsibility for making tea for the rest of the crew.

#012 E2009.3715

BOILING VESSEL

The most important piece of kit in a British armoured vehicle is the Boiling Vessel or 'BV', with the primary purpose of making tea for the crew.

During the Second World War, the morale of soldiers was recorded as 'sinking' when tea became scarce in the North African campaign, and increasing again when more tea was available. The British obsession with tea drinking is well-known, but for soldiers it provides many things – some obvious, some perhaps less so. Tea as a drink helps keep soldiers hydrated and, with sugar, gives energy, too. The caffeine is a stimulant, which is important in keeping people alert. British soldiers in the Desert War also had less dysentery than their German and Italian foes as boiling the water for tea killed bacteria. Making tea is also a ritual and can be a calming process in the stress of war. It brings a familiarity and comfort, and a warming drink. Often, for a tank crew, tea-making is a chance to gather together to drink.

Tank crews have had the advantage over foot soldiers with more capacity to carry tea-making equipment with them. Petrol as a fuel to boil water was readily to hand, water was carried in containers, and small petrol pressure cookers were issued to crews, but these could be temperamental. In the North African campaign, a simple homemade stove was created from the bottom of a 'flimsy' – or tin petrol can – creating an open-topped container. This was filled with petrol-soaked sand. If available, a grate was positioned over this, and the pot or vessel in which to boil water (often the other half of the flimsy) was placed on top. The lit fuel burned and boiled the water, and tea could be made. The improvised stoves were nicknamed 'Benghazi boilers' or cookers and could be used for heating food as well. As soon as a vehicle stopped on campaign, getting a brew on was the task of the loader or hull machine-gunner.

The risk of fire inside the vehicle meant that making tea in the confines of a tank was forbidden, but some crews did do it. By 1945 and the arrival of the Centurion tank, a cooker or Boiling Vessel (BV) was fitted inside the turret. Square in shape, the container plugged into the electrical system of the vehicle. It could contain four tin cans in a water bath. Once the food was heated, the water could be used for drinks or washing, or water could be heated on its own. The BV has been fitted to every British tank since the Centurion, and many other vehicles, too. It is often called the most important piece of equipment in the vehicle. In the First Gulf War, US tank crews were amazed and envious to see British tank crews emerging from their vehicles with a hot brew in hand, and this led to US tanks and vehicles soon afterwards being fitted with a similar device.

A BV can boil water to make a brew or to heat ration pouches and tins. The hot water may also be used for washing with.

#013 E2008.3506

BONE DOME

The AFV-73 tank crewman's 'bone dome' seemed a good idea, integrating head protection and communications, but it was impractical and crews thought it looked silly.

Above: Trooper Milligan of the 4th Royal Tank Regiment sporting the much maligned 'bone dome'. Introduced in 1973, the AFV-73 'bone dome' was unofficially known by some as the 'Dan Dare' helmet or the 'Turnip'.

Below: The rim on the bone dome was found to get in the way when crews put their eyes up to periscopes or sights – a major drawback

Protective equipment for tank crews is obviously important. In 1916, leather helmets were issued to help cushion head blows, then cork helmets in the 1930s and a metal rimless helmet during the Second World War.

In the 1970s, the crewman's helmet or 'bone dome' was issued and proved to be universally unpopular. 'It was, without doubt, the most uncomfortable bit of kit ever. Little short of torture after a couple of hours use. Made of some sort of composite plastic with built-in earphones you could only listen to by wearing,' recalled one veteran. The helmet was large and it got in the way of crew using the sights in tanks like the Chieftain. When first issued, it had a carrying bag and a set of fitting instructions on an attached label.

One problem that took a while to identify was not just the practical elements that seem to fail with the helmet, but the fact crewman felt 'silly' wearing it. Its shape did not flatter the wearer, and in consequence, crews would find reasons not to use the helmet. Head injuries inevitably increased.

The 'look' of kit has always been important to a soldier. The appeal of a uniform alone was crucial to recruiting sergeants for many years. For the modern soldier 'ally kit' is desirable, things that make soldiers look and feel 'cool'. For designers, there is the danger of creating items – such as the bone dome – that soldiers simply do not want to wear because it creates the opposite of 'cool'.

The 'bone dome' or AFV-73 helmet was ultimately replaced in the early 1980s by a much simpler item of headgear, the Combat Vehicle Crewman's Helmet (CVCH) that carried the communication system in a separate removable soft liner.

The AFV-73 'bone dome' was given the official designation 'Helmet-Headset Electrical, A-Vehicle Crewman's Headgear'. It had a communications headset built in, which made the helmet bulkier and was also inconvenient, as it was not always necessary to wear both.

Brangwyn's empathy with stained glass as a medium can be appreciated from the use of colour and line in his treatment of 'The Tank'.

#014 E1976.88

THE TANK
SIR FRANK BRANGWYN RA (1867–1956)

Frank Brangwyn was never an Official War Artist, but he produced dozens of patriotic posters that became synonymous with First World War propaganda.

A watercolour by Sir Frank Brangwyn of *Hyacinth*, a Mark IV 'Male' tank of H Battalion Tank Corps, ditched in the Battle of Cambrai, 20 November 1917.

Brangwyn used a photograph of *Hyacinth* that had been reproduced in magazines and newspapers as inspiration for his work. *Hyacinth* became stuck in a trench just below the village of Ribecourt early in the attack. Brangwyn may have been thinking of the image for a potential poster, but nothing further of this design appeared. Entitled 'The Tank', the painting was exhibited as part of the Brangwyn Exhibition at the Royal Academy, London, in 1952.

Brangwyn came from a creative family; his father was an architect, but he was largely self-taught. At the tender age of 17 he had a painting accepted for the Royal Academy Summer Exhibition and this confirmed him in his choice of an artistic career.

He worked with William Morris on stained glass but became famous in his lifetime for large mural works. Not only a great painter and printmaker, he was also proficient in stained glass, ceramics, furniture design and book illustration. Although never commissioned as an Official War Artist during the First World War, Brangwyn created over 80 striking posters, many to help raise money for charities such as the Red Cross or for encouraging support for War Bond drives.

In the mid-1920s, Brangwyn painted a huge canvas called 'A Tank in Action' as part of his submission for the Royal Gallery in Westminster Palace. Lord Iveagh commissioned the works as a memorial to peers and their relatives killed in the First World War, but the peers judged the pictures as too grim and they were rejected. A later set illustrating the British Empire were also declined but installed in Swansea Guildhall instead. The failure of these commissions to be accepted had a lasting impression on Brangwyn who then started giving away many of his works, including the massive 'A Tank in Action', which he donated to the National Museum of Wales.

The photograph that inspired Brangwyn's watercolour – *Hyacinth* ditched before Ribecourt, 21 November 1917.

#015 E2019.2601

LITTLE AUDREY, ABBESS OF CHANTRY

Good luck charms can take many different forms and are as important to a soldier as his rifle and his mess tin.

Many soldiers take a good luck charm or mascot with them as a reminder of home or loved ones when they head off to battle. Often, they are a simple item like a photograph, a child's drawing or scented handkerchief, but Bill Bellamy was given a rather different mascot.

Bill Bellamy joined the Royal Armoured Corps in December 1941 and served with the 8th King's Royal Irish Hussars between 1943 and 1955. He fought briefly in North Africa and went on to take part in the Normandy landings on D-Day + 2, and the campaign in North West Europe.

Before deploying to Europe, Bellamy's girlfriend at the time, Audrey, gave him this china doll as a good luck charm. Bellamy wrote in his book *Troop Leader, A Tank Commander's Story*, 'She, the doll, was to be my mascot. The troop adopted her without question and my tank, named *Abbot of Chantry*, became known as 'Little Audrey, Abbess of Chantry'. Audrey was attached to the searchlight on the tank's turret and became a very important good luck symbol to the whole troop. Bellamy didn't realise just how much until Audrey was knocked off his tank as he prepared to go into battle in Holland. 'As I was about to give the signal to move, I saw Sergeant Bill Pritchard leap out of his tank, he rushed back to the hedgerow, picked up Audrey, clambered on the back of my tank, handed her to me and shouted "I'm not going without her!" I knew that she had become a very much-loved mascot, but until that moment I hadn't realised the full extent of her role!'

Bill Bellamy wrote about his wartime experiences for his family and gave a copy to The Tank Museum. He later published his account, *Troop Leader*, in 2005, and it has become a classic of tank warfare literature.

Bill Bellamy fought throughout the Battle for Normandy and into the Low Countries as a troop leader in Cromwell tanks.

During the battles in the Normandy Bocage, Bill Bellamy received his first batch of letters from his girlfriend, Audrey. 'Oddly enough at the same time,' he said, 'I found among my kit the china doll which had stood on her dressing table and which she had given to me before we left England.'

#016 E2014.2219

THE BOOK OF COMMON PRAYER

'Defend us thy humble servants in all assaults of our enemies' – Archie Smith's prayer book bears the scorch marks of the fire that destroyed his tank and claimed his life in the Battle of Amiens.

Like so many others, Henry Smith joined the Army in August 1914. Known as 'Archie', he served as a tank gunner in the 1st Company, A Battalion, Tank Corps and he took part in the Battle of Amiens on 8 August 1918. Nine out of 11 tanks in the company were destroyed in the attack and Archie was killed along with the rest of his crew. He was temporarily buried beside his burned-out tank and several years later he was reinterred in the British Cemetery at Bouchoir.

Archie wrote regularly to his younger sister Lilah about his experiences at the Front. On her death in 1983, the letters and this *Book of Common Prayer* with *Hymns A&M* were found among her effects and were donated to The Tank Museum in 2014.

Archie Smith and his sister Lilah. Archie wrote to Lilah of his experiences as a tank crewman.

The prayer book and hymnal was owned by Archie and sent home to Lilah after his death by his friend and fellow Gunner George Boyson. 'I have his prayer book, the only thing we could find because his tank was burnt out. I will send it to you when we get back for a rest,' wrote Boyson in a letter to Lilah Smith in September 1918.

George Boyson was a close friend of Archie Smith and had served with him throughout the war. He helped to bury his friend and later spoke of his deep sense of loss. A photograph of Lilah, burnt in the same way as the prayer book, was also sent home by another friend, Private Thomas Christmas. It is believed to have been with Archie when his tank was set alight and recovered from his body.

#017 E1949.272

MONTY'S BERET

In the Second World War, General Montgomery assumed the black beret of the Royal Tank Regiment as his standard headgear, despite being an infantryman.

After fighting in France with the British Expeditionary Force in 1940, Major General Bernard Montgomery spent two years in Britain, first as a Divisional and then Corps Commander. He had originally been tasked with taking over First Army for Operation 'Torch,' the landings in Morocco, under the overall command of General Dwight D. Eisenhower in the summer of 1942. However, on the morning of 8 August, while shaving at his headquarters in Reigate, he received a phone call from the War Office.

Montgomery instead was to go to Egypt and take command of the Eighth Army. He was more comfortable with this posting: 'I felt I could handle that business, and Rommel,' he declared.

Montgomery was 'hustled out' to Egypt 'at very short notice'. He took over the Eighth Army from the sacked Claude Auchinleck on 15 August 1942. As Montgomery prepared his plans for defeating Rommel, he had to engender a new sense of belief and morale in the Army (Churchill had described the Eighth Army men at this time as

a picture of what was needed and he swiftly 'cancelled all previous orders about withdrawal'. Montgomery had to initially plan a defensive battle to stop Rommel – a battle called Alam Halfa – then prepare his attack. This would become the Second Battle of El Alamein. His plans instilled a sense of conviction and his oft-used phrase, 'grip', in the Eighth Army. Monty purposefully wanted to show his troops that a new man was in charge, and build confidence. He was not beyond using gimmicks – calling men to gather around him for a pep talk, handing out cigarettes (even though he was a non-smoker himself), and he wore a distinctive Australian slouch hat covered in badges. His most famous headgear was a beret given to him by his tank sergeant, Jock Fraser, and later presented to The Tank Museum on 29 September 1945 by Montgomery himself. He wrote:

'This beret was given to me by a Sgt in the RTR, the NCO in command of my tank during the Battle of Alamein in October 1942. It was worn by me from Alamein to Tunis when it was so dirty that I got a new one; it was the Sgt's own beret. I added my General's badge to it and have worn the black beret with two badges ever since.'

Opposite top: General Montgomery wearing his famous beret, from an original painting by E.C. Hill in 1945. Unfortunately, further details about Hill as an artist remain elusive.

Main picture: Monty's black beret showing his general's badge beside that of the Royal Tank Regiment.

'Little Willie' sporting the original type of track that had to be replaced, goes for a test-run outside Lincoln.

#018 E1949.322

'LITTLE WILLIE'
THE FIRST TANK

'Little Willie' is the world's first tank as well as being a ground-breaking British invention – and the oldest armoured fighting vehicle in existence.

The need to find a breakthrough and bring manoeuvre back to a static battlefield led to the development of the tank in the First World War. Britain and France had already used armoured cars and tried experiments with tractors to see if they might be able to cross rough, shell-torn ground and crush barbed wire. Machine-guns were thought to be the main target as they stopped troops advancing. Experiments by the Army and the Navy, spurred by the First Lord of the Admiralty Winston Churchill, led to the formation of the Landships Committee. In July 1915, a contract was given to William Foster & Company of Lincoln (an agricultural machinery manufacturer) to build a tracked machine using imported track from the Bullock Creeping Grip Company of the United States.

Building the vehicle was completed quickly, and a test-run was held on 9 September. The tracks proved the problem and William Tritton – the manager of Fosters, and Walter Gordon Wilson, a serving officer from the Royal Naval Air Service – came up with a solution. They created a pressed steel plate with a flange on the inner side that ran in grooves and stopped the tracks sliding off or dropping away over rough ground. The power came from a Daimler-Knight petrol engine that had been used on large artillery tractors in Britain. Rear wheels fitted to a metal frame were added to assist with steering and the angle of the tracks on the ground.

As a test vehicle, only boiler plate was used as the body, not real armour, and a circular dummy turret was fitted but later removed. The intention was to fit the rotating turret with a 2pdr 'pom pom' gun along with six machine-guns.

Even before 'Little Willie' ran, Wilson and Tritton had thought of a new rhomboid shape for the tank. This new shape would lead to 'Big Willie' or 'Mother', which would evolve to become the Mark I tank that saw action in September 1916.

'Little Willie' (a pun on the name of the Kaiser's son, Crown Prince Wilhelm) took part in demonstrations but was swiftly overtaken in importance by 'Mother'. 'Little Willie' was sidelined and eventually deposited at Bovington, where the vehicle became part of the museum collection.

#019 E2005.1795.1 & E2005.1795.2

FLAGS OF FREEDOM

Citizens of the Italian town of Città Sant'Angelo welcomed their liberators with homemade flags, which they presented to the 8th Royal Tank Regiment.

On 12 June 1944, the Italian hilltop town of Città Sant'Angelo, situated a few miles from Pescara in the Abruzzo region, was liberated by British troops. Days before, partisans had asked all the locals to cooperate with the Allies by showing them where any mines or German positions were hidden. Two local women made flags from scrap material to welcome their liberators – one flag was American, the other a British White Ensign.

After the liberation, a small ceremony was held with the Mayor of Città Sant'Angelo, his wife, the two flag makers and some of the townsfolk.

The flags were handed over to a group of soldiers from B Squadron, 8th Royal Tank Regiment including the Squadron Commander, Major Peter Butt, and Captain Stuart Hamilton.

Hamilton remembered: 'It was a simple but rather moving ceremony and afterwards drinks in celebration were passed around.'

Peter Butt was killed later during fighting for the Gothic Line. The flags were passed to his brother Captain Arthur Butt MC who also served in B Squadron, 8th Royal Tank Regiment, and who donated them to The Tank Museum in the 1980s.

Major Peter Butt and Captain Stuart Hamilton of 8th RTR with the mayor of Città Sant'Angelo, his wife and one of the two flag-makers with the British White Ensign and American stars and stripes. In 1995, Stuart Hamilton MC published *Armoured Odyssey*, his account of the 8th Royal Tank Regiment in the Western Desert, Middle East and Italy between 1941 and 1945.

In common with aircraft instruments, compasses and watches from the First World War until the late 1950s, markings on the P6 compass were painted on using a compound made of copper-doped zinc sulfide and Radium, which reacted by emitting a greenish light. When the zinc sulfide was 'burnt out' after 30 to 50 years it turned orange, but the Radium remains radioactive for a long time, with a half-life of 1,602 years.

#020 E2010.384

P6 COMPASS

Radium paint markings on the P6 compass removed from Peter Vaux's tank glowed in the dark, helping him find his way to the French coast in the retreat of 1940.

The compass displayed here was once part of a Light Mark VI B tank, which took part in the Battle of Arras in 1940. It was taken out of the vehicle by the crew when, during the retreat from the battle, they got lost behind enemy lines. The quotes below are taken from a postwar account written by the tank's commander, Second Lieutenant Peter Vaux.

'I was completely paralysed with fear. Our petrol was almost finished so we made for a wood and deep in the undergrowth hid the tank. We destroyed the wireless set, smashed the guns and generally put the tank out of action. We then removed the P8 (sic) compass, the emergency rations and our greatcoats.'

Over ten days between 21 May and 1 June 1940, Peter Vaux, Major Stewart Fernie and Lance Corporal Robert Burroughs lived on their wits, hiding in farms and woodland in a desperate attempt to escape the notice of the enemy. The plan to reach and cross the river Somme, however, was fraught with setbacks and danger. At one point they were caught by a German officer and Peter Vaux had to shoot him at close range to allow them to escape. By 27 May the three men, lacking food, were exhausted.

'Our morale reached its lowest, hungry, exhausted and disheartened as we were, I think it possible that had I been alone I might have given up… At 1.30am on 1st June we plunged into the river. It was deep, fast-running and we had a bad crossing. Corporal Burroughs was drowned. The Major got across but collapsed on the far bank.

I was swept some 150 yards downstream in a half-dazed condition. I have a clear recollection of Corporal Burroughs drowning, but by this time was too far gone myself to be of any value to him.'

Peter Vaux made it back to Britain and saw long and distinguished service in the Royal Tank Regiment.

Designed originally for aircraft in the 1930s, the P6 was used in RAF fighters like the Supermarine Spitfire and Hawker Hurricane and was converted for use in armoured vehicles. Compasses can be affected by the magnetic field inside a metal tank, so they were tested for use in tanks at Ditton Park, Slough, the Compass Department.

After his evacuation to England Vaux wrote: 'On 5th June we left France and at 6am on 6th June caught our first glimpse of Weymouth Bay. Never, I think have I ever seen anything so beautiful.'

Busts of Hermann Göring were sculpted by many well-known artists of the Third Reich period. They would have been displayed prominently in public buildings and other places worthy of the vain Reichsmarschall.

#021 E1957.8
DAMAGED BUST OF HERMANN GÖRING

This bullet-scarred bronze bust of Reichsmarschall Hermann Göring was among thousands of items of war booty recovered from the ruins of the Third Reich.

This bronze head sculpture of Hermann Göring would have been displayed in Berlin throughout the Second World War. Its destruction is symbolic of the collapse of the Third Reich. Statues and artwork were an important part of Nazi propaganda.

There is some confusion about how the bust got its bullet holes. The first story was presented by Lieutenant Colonel Ambidge in May 1984. He stated that the bust was in the hall of the Kladow Officer's Mess in 1945 and that the bullet holes were made by a drunken Russian soldier on the evening of the British takeover of the barracks on 10 July.

Edward Jackson of the 1st Royal Tank Regiment later recalled finding the head at Detmold. A German officer he spoke to said the holes were made by American soldiers. 'I was with the 1st Royal Tank Regiment in Berlin in 1945. We were stationed in a large Luftwaffe establishment in Detmold. There was a large arms dump, which included guns, aircraft (both Allied and German) and other bits and pieces. I found a large bronze bust of Hermann Göring with two bullet holes, one in the cheek and one on the nose. I kept the bust until the day of demobilisation when I decided it was too heavy to bring home to England. In the meantime, I asked an old German about the bust and he said that the Americans must have made the bullet holes because they captured the camp and they were shooting at just about everything.'

Disfiguring portraits of enemies has a long tradition. Busts from ancient Egypt and Rome have been found to have been systematically vandalised by enemies. To this day, pulling down statues of enemy leaders and disfiguring portraits continues.

An ace fighter pilot in the First World War, Göring was for a time considered a heart-throb to German womanhood. As the Luftwaffe was eclipsed in battle in the Second World War, his power as second to Hitler in the Nazi hierarchy waned.

#022 E1951.7
THE BELSEN WHIP

'The only thing necessary for the triumph of evil is for good men to do nothing' – the Belsen whip is a stark reminder of man's inhumanity to man, and what human beings are capable of doing in the name of an ideology.

Bergen-Belsen Concentration Camp was liberated on 15 April 1945 by the 11th Armoured Division, who were shocked and horrified by what they saw. Many Allied soldiers were encouraged to visit the concentration camps to see first-hand what they had been fighting for. Initially, there had been disbelief that the stories about the camps were true. The famous broadcast by BBC journalist Richard Dimbleby, who had accompanied the troops into Belsen, was simply not believed and his superiors refused initially to broadcast it. 'This day at Belsen was the most horrible of my life,' he later wrote.

The whip is from Belsen. It was used on inmates and was part of the evidence at the Nuremberg

General Percy Hobart (second left), commanding 79th Armoured Division, at Bergen-Belsen Concentration Camp with other officers in front of the billboard erected by British troops that brings home the chilling reality of what had happened inside the camp.

War Trials after the war. These trials took place before an international military tribunal between 1945 and 1949 to prosecute those who had planned, carried out, or otherwise participated in the Holocaust and other war crimes.

In 1951, the whip was given to The Tank Museum by Lieutenant Cartmell, who said it should be kept as evidence as he feared 'a day may come when people will refuse to believe such things as Belsen really happened'.

'Seeing Belsen and the people in it, you realise that you've been up against something pretty horrible,' wrote Bill Wright, 13th/18th Hussars and Staffordshire Yeomanry. 'It was very, very sobering seeing Belsen.'

#023 E1991.70

GOLD-PLATED TANK

This gold-plated Challenger 1 model was commissioned as a gift to the Shah of Iran following the sale of Shir tanks in the 1970s.

This gold-plated model of a Challenger 1 tank was originally crafted as a gift for the Shah of Iran, for his major order of tanks from Britain.

Britain had been a significant exporter of tanks in the 1930s. The Centurion proved a great export success in the 1950s, bringing much needed hard currency to a bankrupt country. Exports of military vehicles helped mitigate the large cost of developing and testing vehicles, and of course factories needed to be kept occupied if staff were to be paid.

The Shah was keen to make his Army the most powerful in the Middle East. In 1971, his Iranian Defence Ministry negotiated a deal with Britain under an MOD-owned company called International Military Services (IMS) to buy a series of tanks worth £387m. The Iranians bought 707 Chieftain tanks, bridgelayers and Armoured Recovery Vehicles, which were delivered in 1978. An improved version of the Chieftain tank (FV 4030/1) was also ordered along with 125 Shir 1 tanks (FV4030/2), and 1,225 examples of the Shir 2 tank (FV4030/3). The Shir 1 tank was being built and the Shir 2 tank's development was almost complete when in 1979 the Shah was deposed from office and a new Revolutionary Government took control. In February they cancelled the huge tank order.

Britain was able to sell 274 Shir 1 tanks to Jordan, renamed as the 'Khalid'. Britain's own replacement for the Chieftain tank was cancelled in 1980 for being too costly and complex, so it took over the Shir 2 tank programme and with a number of adjustments, converted these into what would be the Challenger tank.

The gold tank was a gift made for the Shah in thanks for his impressive tank order. With the order cancelled, the tank was given to The Tank Museum in 1991. A larger problem was the demand by the new Iranian Revolutionary Government for the return of the money for the cancelled tank programme. The dispute over this money rumbled on until 2022 when repayment was finally made.

This Challenger 1, *Churchill*, was used by Lieutenant Colonel Arthur Denaro, Commanding Officer of the Queen's Royal Irish Hussars during the Gulf War of 1990-91, and is now part of The Tank Museum collection.

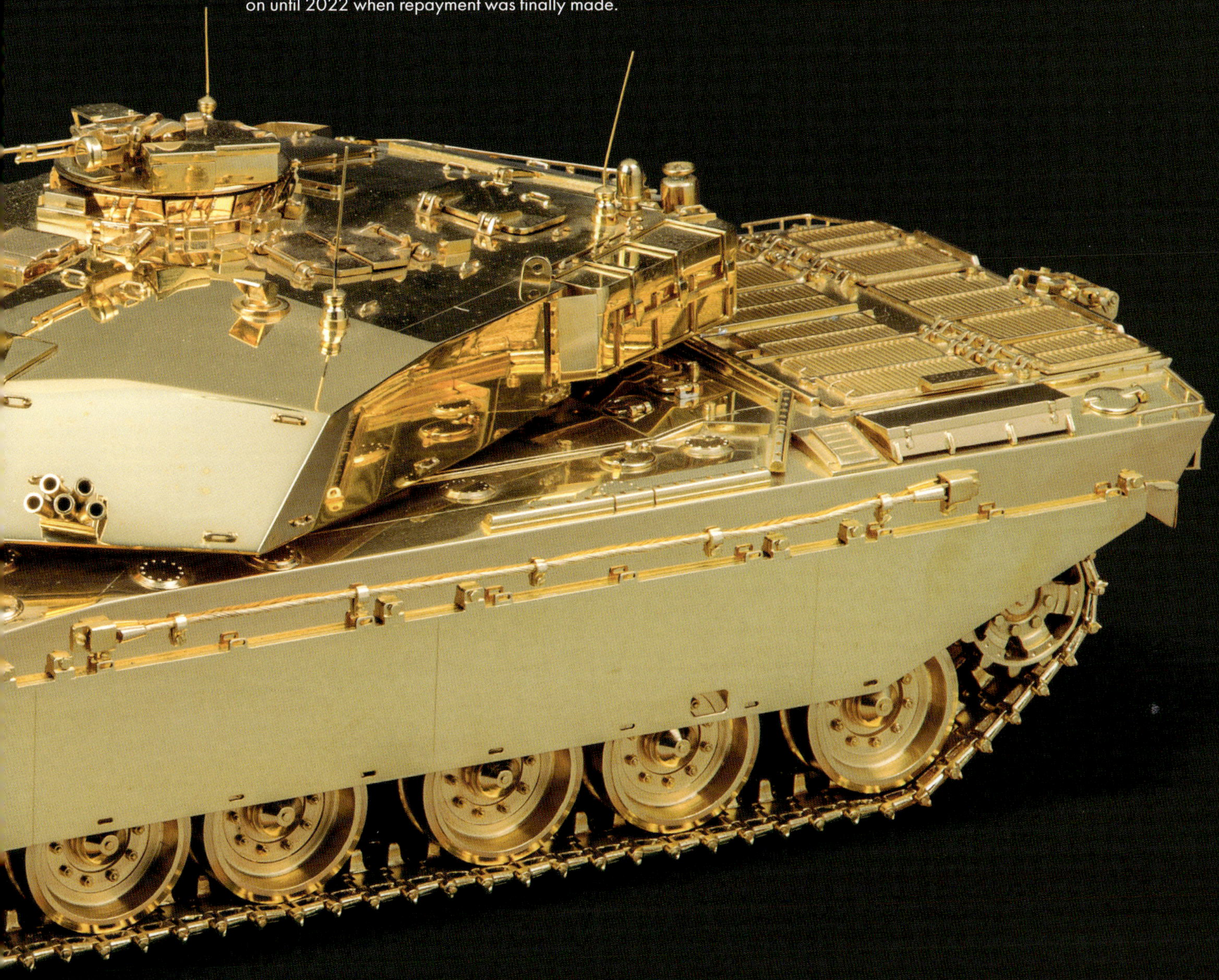

#024 E2003.933

LANCE CORPORAL CHARLES NYE'S SINGLE-SHOT PISTOL

This odd little pistol was ineffective at anything but point-blank range, but had the advantage of being easily concealed, which helped Charles Nye escape from his captors.

This single-shot Derringer-type pistol could fire a short .22 bullet. It was a type readily available for commercial purchase and was produced in huge quantities by the Belgian gun factories around Liège in the 19th and early 20th Centuries. It was donated to the museum in 2003.

Britain has a strong reputation today of having a very small and controlled gun culture, but this certainly was not always the case. Weaponry to defend oneself or property had been established in law as early as King Henry VIII's reign.

The police had access to guns, but for most of the 19th and 20th centuries they did not carry them, having truncheons issued instead. In late-Victorian Britain this led to occasions when the police asked the public to borrow weapons to return fire on armed criminals.

As the 20th Century progressed the number of firearms in private ownership became steadily more controlled and regulated. By 1946, when a gun amnesty saw 75,000 weapons handed in over six weeks, self-protection was no longer considered an acceptable reason to hold a gun.

This pistol was given to Lance Corporal Charles Nye of the Machine Gun Corps by his grandmother, who had carried it on her rounds as a midwife in the tough area of Wood Green, London, before the First World War.

Nye kept the pistol concealed in his Brodie helmet. When he was captured on the Western Front, he used the pistol to shoot his guard and escape together with at least one other man. After his escape, Nye was subsequently wounded in both legs and invalided back to Netley Abbey Military Hospital near Southampton.

Charles Nye of the Machine Gun Corps.

#025 E2010.1237

SIGHT FROM MAUS

Despite the sheer size of the 188-ton *Maus*, it is doubtful if it would have been much of an asset for Nazi Germany had it entered production.

Above: The *Maus* was one of the largest tanks ever designed but it was never completed, even in its prototype form.

Main picture: After the defeat of Germany, Britain and the Allies conducted a systematic search for information on weaponry, production techniques and technology. Paperwork, designs and examples of the materials and items captured were returned to Britain for study. The *Maus* sight was probably brought here as part of this project.

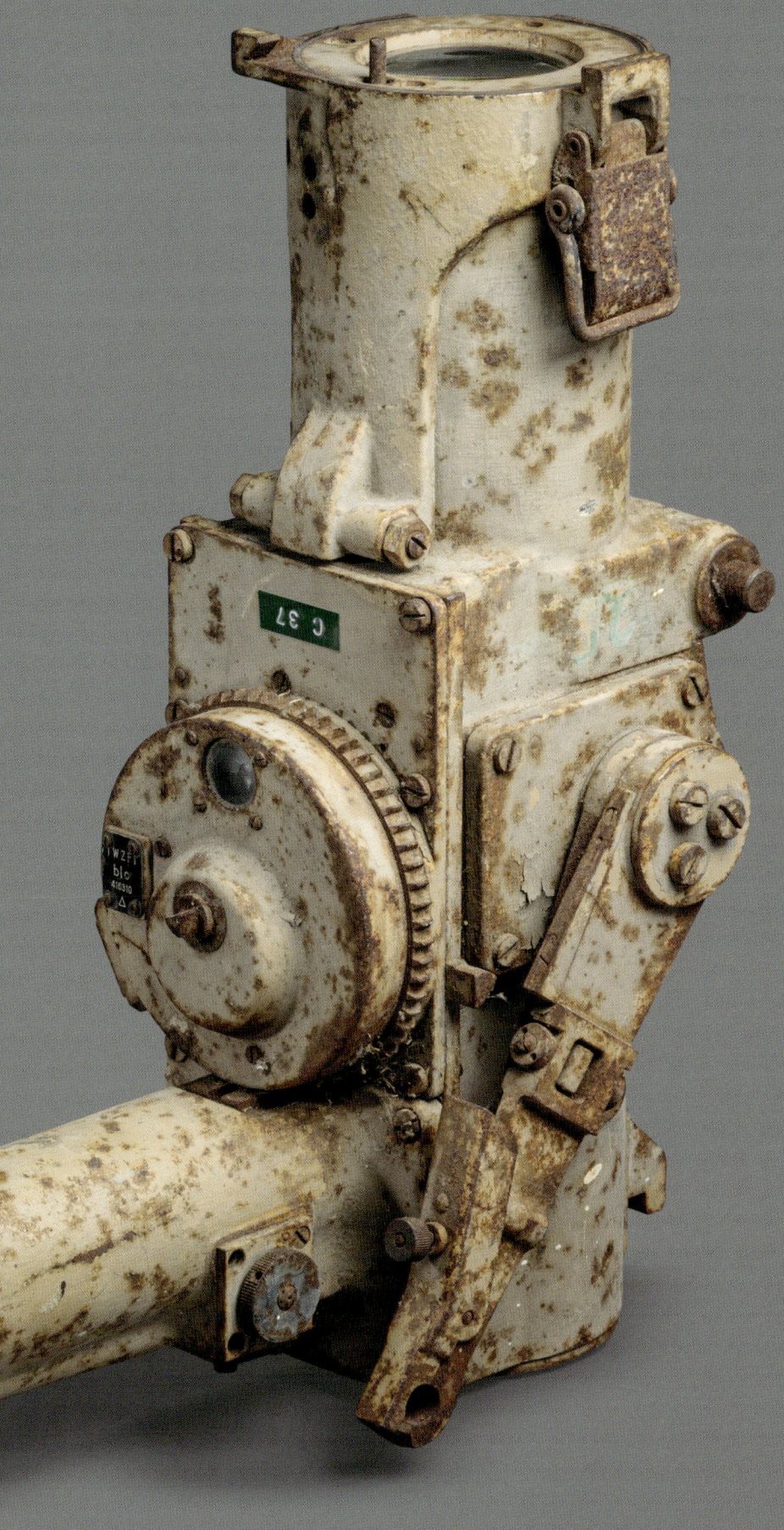

The desire to build super-heavy tanks for the German military came from Adolf Hitler himself. First mention of a possible 100-ton Panzer appears in minutes of a meeting between Hitler and Albert Speer, the Reich Armaments Minister, in March 1942. Hitler saw the need for super-heavy tanks as he thought the Red Army would field even bigger tanks in the spring of 1943. The KV-1 and T-34 had been shock enough for the German military when they had invaded the Soviet Union in the summer of 1941.

In January 1943, Hitler selected a Porsche-proposed design for the *Panzerkampfwagen 'Maeuschen'* or *'Maus'* as the vehicle was known. Weight increases (the tank came in at 188 tons) meant Porsche had to design a new suspension system for the *Maus*. There were delays with materials and equipment supplies despite Hitler's keenness to see the project progress.

Holes cut in the front armour not only take time and engineering resources to complete, but they also weaken the level of protection the armour provides to a vehicle. This is probably the reason why a *Kippspiegel-Zielfernrohr*, or periscopic gunsight, was fitted. As you faced the tank, the gunner would sit on the right of the turret and the sight he used was covered by an armoured cone on the front right of the turret roof. The cut-out aperture in the cone allowed the sight to see from -7 to + 23 degrees.

Zeiss are recorded as having delivered a model of the sight to the *Maus* project in June 1943 for incorporation in the wooden turret mock-up. This sight, marked as *TWZF1*, is the sight fitted for the main armament on the *Maus*, a 12.8cm main gun. The sight has the three-letter code 'blc', which indicates Carl Zeiss as the manufacturer.

Bombing raids on the Krupp factory in March and August 1943 led to a report estimating a further seven-month delay in production. This resulted in a decision in October to cancel all *Maus* production and concentrate resources on the production of other vehicles. Only two prototype vehicles were completed and these were blown up before the advancing Red Army in 1945.

A turret and a hull from the wrecked vehicles were saved and a hybrid vehicle was created, which is now on display in Moscow.

#026 E1970.20.2

MARK I TANK

The British Mark I was the first ever tank to see combat. Out of 150 built, The Tank Museum has the last surviving example.

This Mark I tank was presented to Lord Salisbury in 1919. It was displayed at his Hatfield Park estate in Hertfordshire to commemorate the use of his grounds for some of the earliest tank demonstrations in 1916. In 1969 it came to The Tank Museum when it was realised it was the last remaining Mark I. It has been repainted to represent the tank *Clan Leslie* as it appeared during the first attack on the Somme on 15 September 1916, with a replica of the 'bomb-proof' net roof, rear steering wheels taken from a Mark II and replica longer 6pdr guns made of wood.

After the trials of 'Little Willie' and then the more successful 'Mother' in January 1916, the production of the Mark I went ahead. Of the 150 tanks being built, half were male with 6pdr guns, and half were female with twin Vickers machine-guns in the side sponsons.

The first attack with the tanks was not a resounding success but the British Commander-in-Chief, Douglas Haig, saw enough potential in the tank to order more. Mark I tanks were used in small numbers later in the year. The rear wheels were removed as they had little effect, and improvements were made with stronger brakes and track rollers.

Eight Mark I tanks were sent to Palestine and saw action at the Battle of Gaza. Newer models were in preparation and the last 15 Mark Is took part in

One of the first tanks to attack in September 1916 was a Mark I, C13 *Clan Leslie*, seen in Chimpanzee Valley behind the British frontline on the Somme.

the Battle of Arras in April 1917. Those Mark I tanks that remained were converted into supply tanks.

There were many critics of the Mark I being used in what they saw as a premature way. Winston Churchill thought they should have been built in larger numbers for a more effective attack, and the French argued for the attack to be held off until their own tank programme was ready. Haig, however, was under huge pressure to see some success after the costly summer battles and it is perhaps understandable that he would use any resources available to him, including testing his new weapon.

The actual wartime history of this Mark I is as yet unknown – and it suffered from decades of exposure outside – but a clue may yet emerge to help identify the vehicle.

#027 E2016.2690

DINKY No 651 CENTURION TANK

With a fully rotating turret, rubber tracks and measuring 5¾ inches in length, the Dinky Centurion tank was a popular toy in the 1950s and 60s.

Frank Hornby (1863–1936) was responsible for three great toy brands – Meccano, Hornby Toy Railways and Dinky Toys. He started with Mechanics Made Easy in 1902 – a product that became Meccano in 1907. As early as 1915, Hornby started making toy tinplate railway carriages, which would lead to the famous 0 and 00 gauge model railways. In the early 1930s, vehicles were made to add to station scenery. These were called Hornby Modelled Miniatures and later in 1934 Meccano Dinky Toys.

The first set of Dinky toys (22 a to f in production serial codes) included a lead tank with a coloured turret that did not represent any real tank. Later, Hornby started making zinc alloy toy cars that would be known as 'Dinkys' or Dinky Toys.

Military vehicles were made from 1937 and included a set of Royal Tank Corps soldiers and a set of Mechanised Force vehicles. Metal wire tracks were fitted to the model Medium tank (151a) and a Dragon artillery tractor. The Second Word War stopped production but some models were released from stocks for sale each Christmas. The Medium tank model was made again after the war from 1947 to 1952.

Dinky made a Centurion tank (651) from 1954 to 1970. It originally cost seven shillings and eleven pence (7/11d) – a fairly expensive toy when pocket money for a child might be sixpence. The tank's barrel could get bent by stepping on and the black rubber track could perish and snap, but it was a favourite toy that many of a certain age still have saved.

The real thing: this Centurion sports the later model of the 20pdr gun with a fume extractor halfway along the barrel.

The Dinky Centurion tank has become a collector's item more than 50 years after the model ceased production in 1970.

#028 E1949.200

TANK CAMOUFLAGE MODEL
PERCYVAL TUDOR-HART (1873 – 1954)

Canadian artist Percyval Tudor-Hart specialised in colour theory and offered his services to the War Office to create camouflage schemes, but his innovative designs were ultimately rejected.

The French word camouflage had not been used in Britain before the First World War, but it soon became known not just to the military, but to the general public. Camouflage became a popular topic in magazines and *Punch* cartoons.

Percyval Tudor-Hart was from a wealthy Canadian family and studied in Paris before opening an art school there. He sculpted and painted with bold colours, taking a particular interest in colour theory. Moving to London, his new art school had to close at the beginning of the First World War as students disappeared into military service. Determined to assist with the war effort, Tudor-Hart's biographer stated that as he 'possessed of specialised knowledge of colour and colour values' he decided his best contribution would be 'in the realm of scientific camouflage, based on the reflection, absorption, and refraction of light'.

Tudor-Hart offered his services to the War Office and was invited by Lord Montagu of Beaulieu to set up a workshop at Warren Farm on his estate. He managed to have a number of his previous students released from military service to assist him and gained a grant of £500 from Sir Alfred Mond, First Commissioner of Works. The Air Board turned down his suggestions for aeroplane camouflage and this triggered a series of disappointments in which all the services, Navy, Army and air forces ultimately rejected Tudor-Hart's schemes. In January 1917, he was supplied with two model tanks to paint – we assume this model is one of those supplied – to show off his suggested camouflage design. He visited Bovington as part of his work with tanks.

Tudor-Hart was asked to become an advisor to the Special Works (Camouflage) School in Kensington Gardens. His design for a camouflaged sniper suit was trialled on the frontline and found satisfactory, but another design had already been accepted for use.

This large model, made of wood and canvas, has been heavily repaired but shows Tudor-Hart's herringbone paint effect. There was a sister model with a camouflage scheme attributed to Solomon J. Solomon. This scheme was painted on the Mark I tanks, but records show this model was destroyed in the 1960s as 'beyond repair'.

Opposite top: One of Tudor-Hart's schemes is tested on a female tank. The roof structure was presumably meant to carry further camouflage.

Main picture: Although an actual tank was painted in this herringbone camouflage pattern, it was never used in combat. In any event, it was soon found that the tanks just ended up covered in mud so most were simply painted brown.

#029 E1949.329

ROLLS-ROYCE
1920-PATTERN ARMOURED CAR

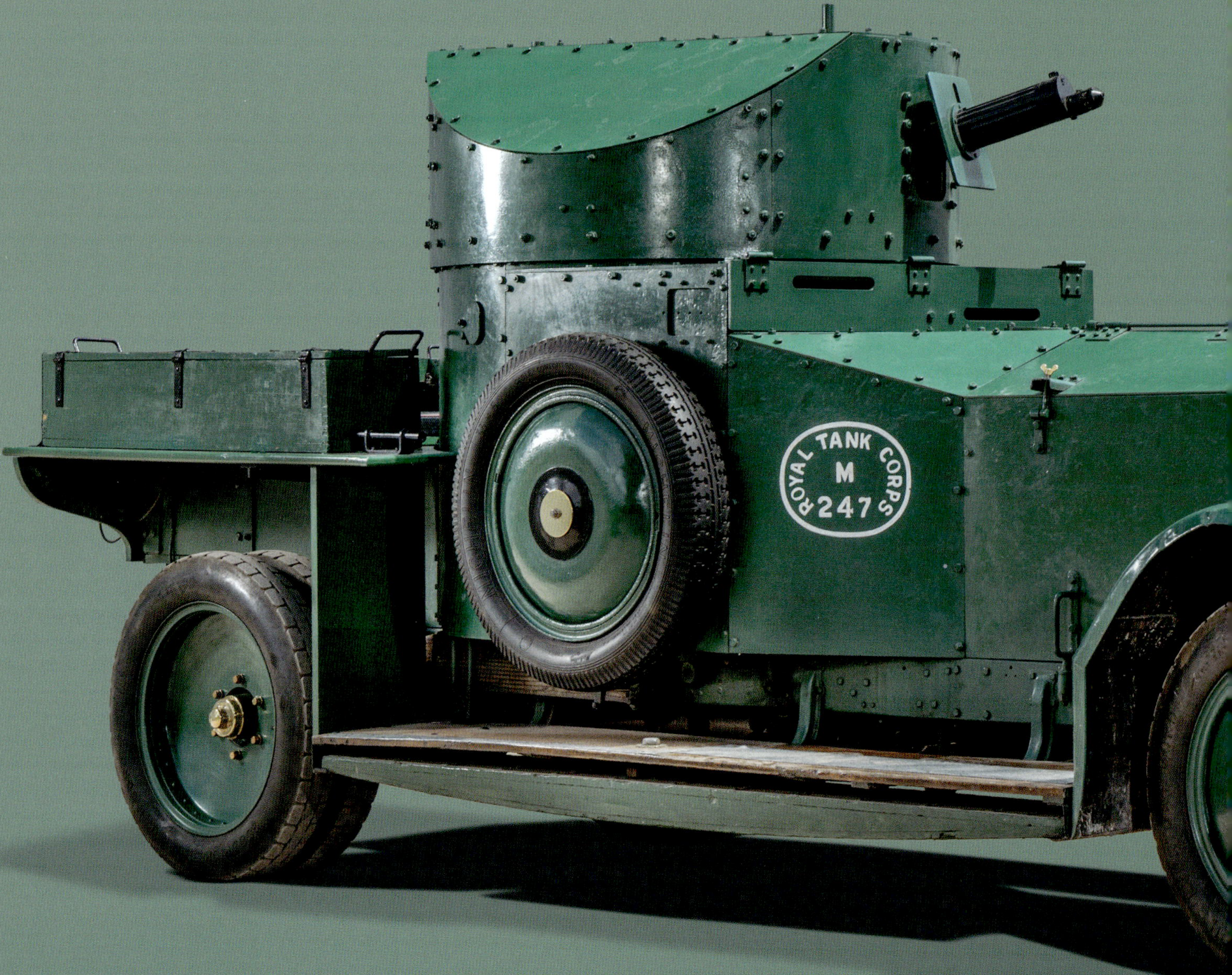

The Rolls-Royce armoured car is the oldest running vehicle in The Tank Museum's collection. It has seen service across the world, from Scarborough to Shanghai.

It was the Royal Navy that raised the first Armoured Car Squadron in 1914, seeing the need for armoured cars to protect air bases in France and Belgium in the period before the more static trench lines were established. Rolls-Royce Silver Ghost cars were requisitioned, and the Admiralty Air Department designed an armoured hull and a rotating turret to contain a .303in Vickers machine-gun.

The first few examples were delivered in December 1914, just as the mobile period of warfare ended. Squadrons of 12 vehicles were set up by the Royal Naval Air Service and these six squadrons were handed over to the Army in August 1916. On the Western Front they had little chance to see useful action, but in the Middle East they were able to manoeuvre and saw extensive service. T.E. Lawrence famously said the nine Rolls cars that served with him were 'more valuable than rubies', and he had a lifelong love for the car.

A new improved pattern of the car was built in 1920 with thicker armour plate on the radiator and a new wheel type. Further improvements came in 1924 with a new turret and commander's cupola. A version with lengthened hull armour and a larger domed turret with four machine-gun mounts was built for service in India.

The Tank Museum's 1920-pattern car, F247, is now over 100 years old. It was issued to the Tank Corps' 5th Armoured Car Company in Ireland before it moved to Scarborough in March 1923. In January 1927, it went to Shanghai and later served in Egypt before returning to Britain.

F247 came to the museum just after the Second World War and has been maintained in running order. In May 1997, it provided transport for Her Majesty Queen Elizabeth II when she visited Bovington and has led a parade down the Mall in London.

It somehow seems wrong to give weapons of war warming descriptions – but the Rolls-Royce Armoured Car has a stately presence and elegance that over time has bewitched not just visiting public, but a number of workshop staff who have had the task of looking after this classic machine.

#030 E1949.330
VICKERS MEDIUM MARK II

Perhaps the most important British tank to never fire a shot in anger, the Vickers Medium was used between the wars to experiment with the role of armour on the battlefield.

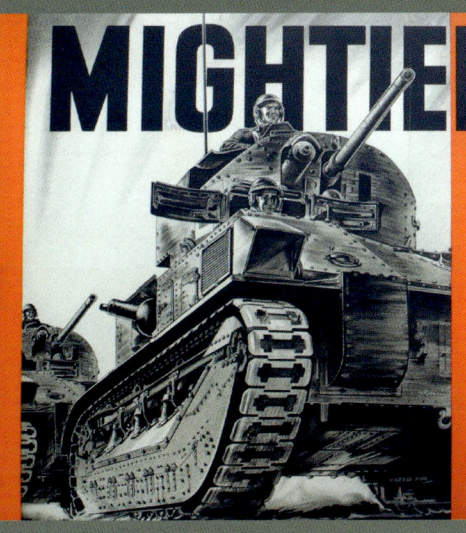

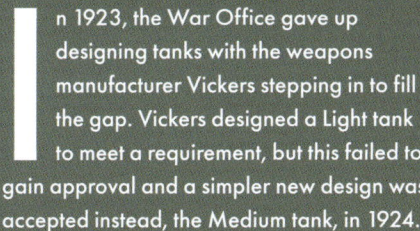

'Mightier Yet!' featuring Vickers Medium Mark II tanks is one of a series of posters from early in the Second World War lauding the British armed forces. Its artist, Harold A. Pym (1915–79), is best known for his poster artwork and he produced many designs for the Ministry of Information during the war including specifically for the 'Salute the Soldier' campaign.

In 1923, the War Office gave up designing tanks with the weapons manufacturer Vickers stepping in to fill the gap. Vickers designed a Light tank to meet a requirement, but this failed to gain approval and a simpler new design was accepted instead, the Medium tank, in 1924.

The Mark II version was built between 1925 and 1934, and had protected suspension, a higher vision port for the driver and a new hull shape. All the Vickers Mediums displayed advanced features and yet also had design weaknesses. For ease of maintenance, the 90hp Armstrong Siddeley air-cooled engine sat beside the driver at the front, the gearbox was beneath the commander's feet and the final drive wheel was at the rear. However, this was considered a backward step as even in later First World War tanks, the engine was being compartmentalised away from the crew to help with safety and reduce noise.

The real advantage of the tank was its three-man turret. This meant the commander could get on with commanding the tank and not have to act as a loader, as was the case in most two-man turrets. The tank carried a 3pdr (47mm) gun and ball mounts for Hotchkiss (later Vickers) machine-guns. Some 200 Mediums were manufactured and allowed Britain to carry out influential experiments in the interwar period – learning the potential of what armoured formations could achieve. They were crewed by the Royal Tank Corps and were often used to portray the forward-looking nature of the British Army in recruiting posters and the press.

These tanks did see some action on the Indian North West Frontier in 1935, but most had been phased out of operational use by the outbreak of the Second World War.

#031 E2002.1031

CORPORAL STEPHEN KENNEDY MM
MALCOLM McGREGOR
(1934 – 2010)

Illustrator Malcolm McGregor's repertoire covered a wide range of subjects for children's and adult books, ranging from wild animals to army uniforms.

Malcolm McGregor studied this photograph of General Montgomery with his Grant tank crew for this illustration of Corporal Stephen Kennedy (third from left).

This illustration shows a British tank soldier, copied from the photograph seen on the opposite page. It was painted in watercolour, gouache and ink by Malcolm McGregor in the early 1970s as a commission for *The Elite* magazine. McGregor also made similar illustrations for a book called *Army Uniforms of World War Two*. The text was written by his long-term collaborator Andrew Mollo – a uniforms expert who worked as an advisor on a number of films such as *Doctor Zhivago* and *The Eagle has Landed,* and on the *Sharpe* television series.

Malcolm McGregor grew up in London during the Blitz; this influenced his passion for military subjects and he trained as a commercial illustrator. His style of meticulous detail was well suited to reproducing the impression of fabrics, leather and webbing as can be seen here.

For the purposes of this illustration McGregor researched the person in the photograph, Cpl (later Sgt) Stephen Kennedy MM of B Squadron, 6th Royal Tank Regiment, 7th Armoured Division. The picture was taken on 6 November 1942, and McGregor noted he was part of the crew of Montgomery's Grant tank.

'Commercial art' has traditionally been viewed as a much inferior art form from high or 'gallery' works, however skilled the producer. The commercial process sees the commissioning of the artwork to illustrate a magazine, book or sales product. As soon as the image has been reproduced, it is discarded or returned to the artist having served its purpose. Very few commercial artists became famous for their work – Norman Rockwell is a rare exception. Malcolm McGregor did sell some of his illustrations, but donated this image and a number of other tank crew illustrations to The Tank Museum in 2002. Sadly, by then, as a brilliant illustrator, he was losing his eyesight.

#032 E1951.23

TIGER 131

The Tank Museum's Tiger I is the only running example anywhere in the world today. Some 80 years after it rolled off the production line, it still exudes strength and power.

This Tiger tank left the Henschel Factory in Kassel, Germany, in February 1943, with serial number 250122 (production started with 250001). It was issued to the newly formed 504th Heavy Tank Battalion whose commander, Major August Seidensticker, had been appointed on 8 February. He departed for Tunisia on 13 March to try to ascertain how his new unit would be employed.

Tiger 131 (131 signifying 1st Company, 3rd Platoon, first tank in the platoon) travelled through Italy, across the straits of Messina to Sicily and then across the Mediterranean to Tunis in March 1943. The tank was captured intact on 24 April on hilly ground at Point 174. Battle damage from its short service life can still be seen on the vehicle. Some damage, such as a smashed loader's hatch and dented roof above the driver and co-driver position has been repaired. As the first complete Tiger tank to be captured in the West it was used for a recognition film and subject to a series of detailed reports analysing its capabilities and characteristics. Winston Churchill and King George VI saw the tank in Tunisia, and on its arrival in Britain it was shown off on Horse Guards Parade in London. Tiger 131 went through firing trials at Lulworth and was taken apart for analysis at Chertsey. In 1951, the incompletely re-assembled tank (the original engine had been taken out and sectioned as a teaching aid) was given to The Tank Museum along with many other captured vehicles.

Always a popular exhibit, the reputation of the Tiger tank, fearsome in wartime, seemed to grow in significance and popularity after the war. The Tank Museum became part of this story as it restored the tank to running order with help from the Heritage Lottery Fund, other funding bodies and supporters. The museum created a series of events to show off the Tiger and in 2013 the tank was filmed alongside another museum vehicle, a Sherman M4A2, for the film *Fury*.

Some 1,354 Tiger I tanks were made and despite displaying a leap forward in gun size and protection, the overall numbers manufactured were small when compared to T-34 or Sherman tank production. In consequence, the Tiger had less real effect on the battlefield than its reputation justifies. When standing in front of the tank, however, it is easy to see why the myth of invincibility is hard to challenge.

Tiger 131 on the day of its capture. The interest in the new tank, the first complete example seized in the West, can be clearly seen in this photograph.

#033 E1991.50.1
CARRIERS IN PRODUCTION AT THE FORD MOTOR COMPANY
HELEN McKIE (1889–1957)

Ford opened its massive vehicle production plant at Dagenham in 1931, replacing the company's earlier UK factory at Trafford Park in Manchester.

Many companies were keen to record their wartime contributions to the war effort and a number of histories were written in the immediate postwar era. Ford commissioned a book called simply *Ford at War* and commissioned Hilary St George Saunders to write the text and Helen McKie to illustrate it. This large watercolour and ink picture is reproduced on page 82 of the book and shows the production of Universal Carriers.

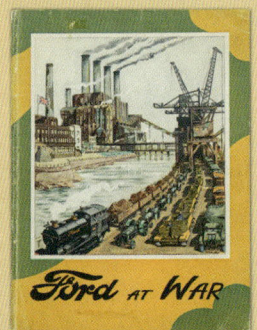

Ford at War was published in 1946. Its author Hilary St George Saunders also wrote books and pamphlets for the Ministry of Information during the Second World War.

led to a praising article in the *Hippodrome Magazine* saying 'her many military types – from the characteristic and humorous point of view – have won for her the sobriquet of "The Soldiers' Friend"'.

Despite her light-hearted portrayal of the military, McKie lost her 24-year-old brother, Douglas, who died of wounds after the Battle of Arras in 1917.

McKie's style was bright and breezy, which was excellent for posters. She produced a number for the Southern Railway, as well as book covers, story illustrations and decorative murals. Of the latter, she was commissioned to create several murals at some of Butlin's Holiday Camps, at Selfridges in London, and the Ford plant at Dagenham – where this painting was completed.

Helen McKie studied at Lambeth School of Art and became a successful commercial artist, being commissioned to create illustrations for magazines such as *The Graphic*, *Sphere* and *Autocar*. She worked for *The Bystander* magazine from 1915–29 at a time when it employed some of the best illustrators and cartoonists in the country. The famous 'Old Bill' cartoons by Bruce Bairnsfather were published in *The Bystander* along with works by H.M. Bateman and W. Heath Robinson. The influence of Bairnsfather can be seen in her early work. She often portrayed soldiers, which

The prominent position of the woman in the factory setting is no accident. Just as the First World War had seen women take over so many traditionally male roles in society, the British effort in the Second World War relied heavily on women's labour.

Some 5,100 Universal Carriers were built in Ford's Essex factory on the marshes bordering the River Thames, which represented a small proportion both of the total number of Carriers (over 110,000) and total wartime vehicle production at Dagenham (355,000).

#034 E1955.74

BESA MACHINE-GUN

Like the Bren gun, the BESA was a license-built version of a Czech-designed weapon.

Britain purchased licences to build weapons from a number of Czechoslovakian manufacturers in the late 1930s as part of its rearmament programme. Perhaps the most famous was the ZB 26 machine-gun, designed and built by the state-owned Zbrojovka Brno factory. With alterations this was manufactured in the UK as the Bren gun (Bren = BR from ZB's home in Brno, EN from Enfield where the Royal Small Arms Factory was located).

Another example was the ZB 53 machine-gun designed by Václav Holek for Zbrojovka Brno. It was used in many of Czechoslovakia's border fortifications and as secondary armament in Czech-built tanks. An agreement was reached for the Birmingham Small Arms Company (BSA) to manufacture the gun under licence in the UK as the BESA, its primary purpose to be fitted to armoured vehicles.

In the late 1930s the War Office had intended British service ammunition to move from rimmed to rimless cartridges, but with war seemingly approaching this was abandoned as a bad idea. The conversion of the ZB 53 to .303in ammunition was also considered too time consuming and complex, so the decision was made to retain the original calibre of 7.92mm. As the gun would be used on vehicles manned by the Royal Armoured Corps alone it was thought the supply of a different ammunition type would not be a problem. There was also the possibility of reusing captured German 7.92mm ammunition.

Too bulky to remove from the tank and use in a ground-mounted role, the gun needed a large aperture cut in the armour in order for it to be mounted. The requirement for a vertical face in which to place the hull machine-gun mount led to the stepped front on the Churchill, Cromwell and Comet tanks,

The BESA was a reliable weapon. It went through a series of improvements to simplify its manufacture, leading to seven 7.92mm variants being kept in service until the mid-1960s with 39,332 made.

A BESA machine-gun training mount. The flat vertical face of the gun mount can be clearly seen.

#035 E2008.4721

SEALED PATTERN WASHER

From the largest gun to the smallest widget, everything used by the Army had an approved example labelled and 'sealed' for use as a standard for look and quality.

The British military used, and uses, a vast range of uniforms, badges and equipment. This material, for understandable reasons, needs to meet certain standards or approved designs. For many decades, key items that had been approved had an example 'sealed'. This meant the item was labelled and 'sealed' ready to be used as a standard for look and quality.

In earlier days a Pattern Room in Whitehall held the sealed pattern. Further copies of 'approved patterns' were sent to the relevant units in the case of badges or insignia, and 'approved' or 'master patterns' were held at the relevant purchasing agencies. Master patterns could be loaned to copy by manufacturers and an approved regimental tailor might need a sample to initially copy for uniforms. Examples of weapons, or small arms below .50-calibre, were held at Enfield Lock, home of the Royal Small Arms Factory until its closure. The collection now resides at the Royal Armouries in Leeds.

Items had an identification label tied to them and a wax seal on cotton tapes was impressed with a 'Board of Ordnance' seal. In the 1980s these wax seals were replaced by a lead seal on nylon cord.

No matter how small and humble, this washer was retained as a master pattern. It was used on portable cookers and was first approved in 1942 as a standard fit for use. It shows a series of records where it was re-approved for use on multiple occasions – the last in 1968. It was disposed of with other items by the Ministry of Defence in 2009.

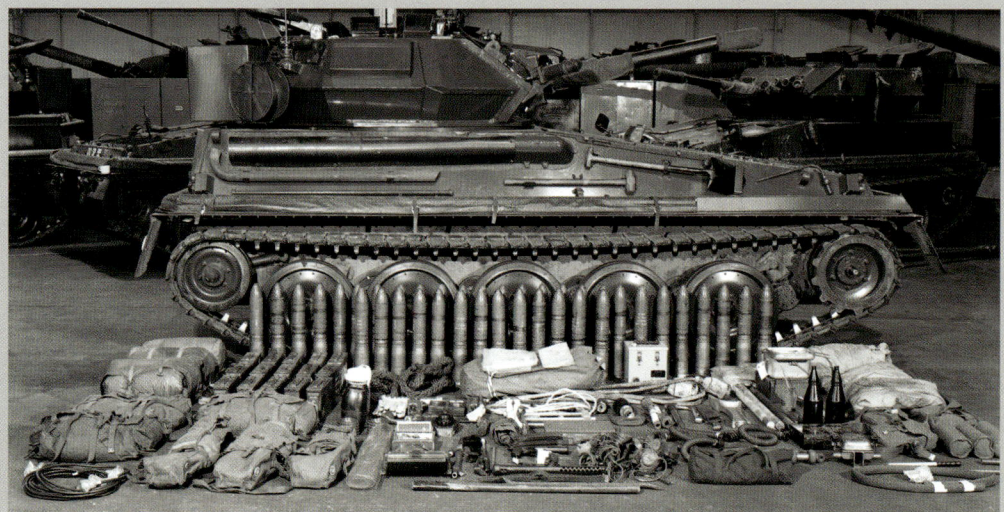

A vehicle carries a huge amount of kit and is itself made up of thousands of parts, all of which have to meet some form of standard. Here is the stowage carried by a Scorpion light tank.

The identification label with wax seal for the humble portable cooker washer.

#036 E2009.5624
TANK SUIT

The one-piece Oversuit (Tank Crews) or 'Pixie' suit was introduced in 1944 and proved popular with wearers.

What to wear in a tank has always been an issue for the crew. For practical purposes the clothes need to be comfortable, adjustable, give protection from the climate and conditions inside and outside the vehicle. The clothes also have to be designed with the need to exit the vehicle quickly and allow an injured crewman to be removed from a cramped interior.

Black uniforms (to hide obvious grease) were adopted by the Royal Tank Corps in the late 1920s, but overalls were also worn as many crew activities were inevitably dirty ones. During the war, appropriate safety clothing for crews was set as a task for a committee based at Lulworth led by a Canadian, Dr Omond McKillop Solandt. The AFV crewman's helmet was suggested by this committee.

Crews were issued with simple tan-coloured overalls in the North African campaign, but efforts at creating flame-retardant clothing came to nothing. Because of the slow progress the Director Royal Armoured Corps ordered a series of three

Left The Oversuit (Tank Crews) in heavyweight light khaki cotton features two rows of zippers fastening from neck to ankle and seven external patch pockets. Adjustment tabs are fitted to ankles and cuffs.

Opposite: In this back view the hood, waist belt and full-cut seat for comfort when sitting down are evident. Internally, the suit is lined and is provided with integral support braces to hold up the trouser legs when the upper suit was removed for heavy work like track bashing.

76 THE TANK MUSEUM IN 100 OBJECTS

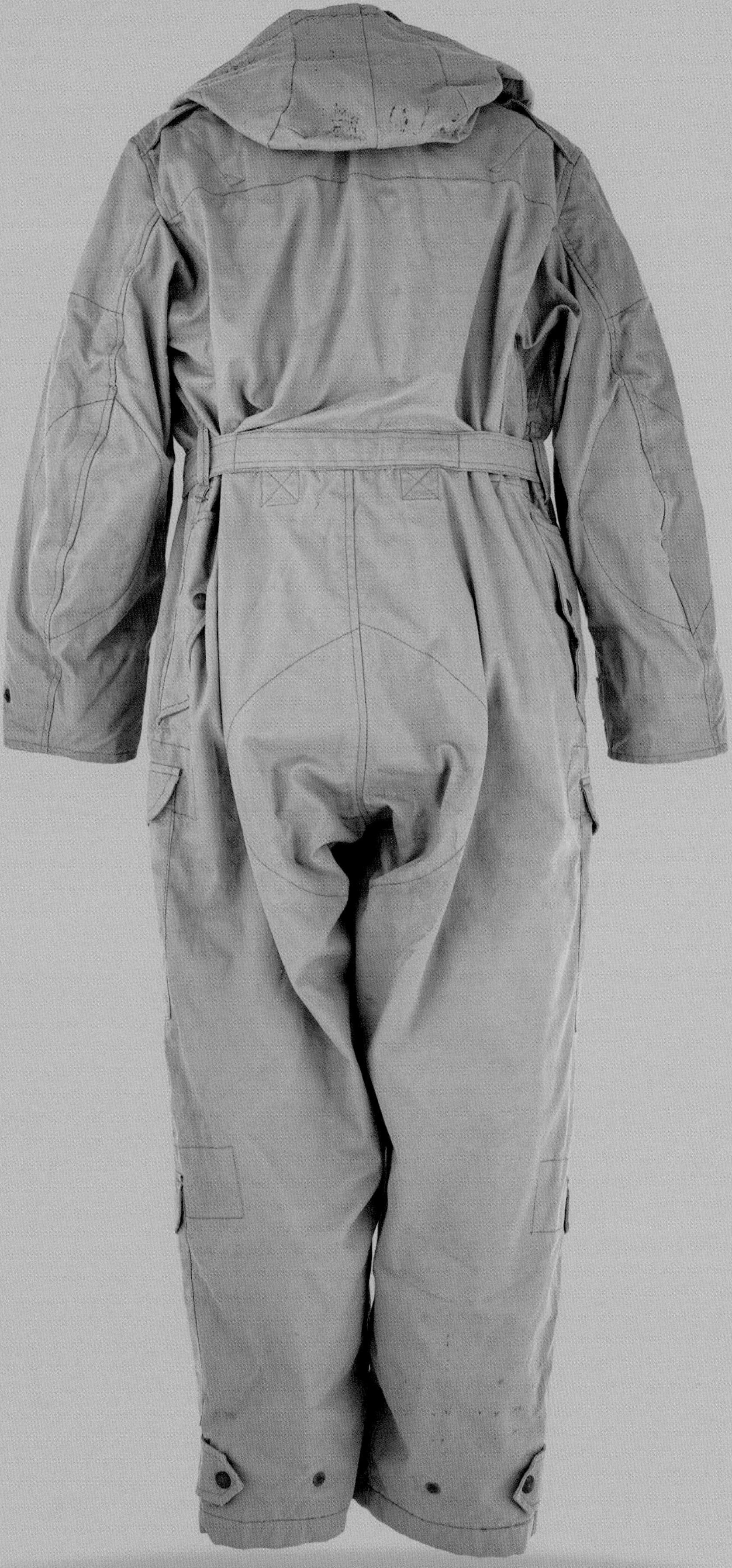

A Sherman Crab flail tank crew in North West Europe during the winter of 1944/45. The Tank Suit is worn by three of the crew members; the others wear leather jerkins.

tank suits, which seem to have been designed at the same time, but were put into production when needed. The first to be manufactured was a green denim suit for use in temperate climates. It was issued in the spring of 1944 and can be seen being used in the Normandy campaign.

In September a new type of suit called an Oversuit – Tank Crews (seen here) was issued. The suit ended up with a number of nicknames including Zoot suit, Pixie suit and Zip suit. Prototypes of the new suit were first trialled a year before issue in Exercise 'Dracula', when Allied tanks were being road-tested in Britain during August and September 1943. The suit proved popular as it was warm, being lined with blanket material, and had rubberised cotton on the upper facing surfaces to give some weather protection. It could be zipped up in a manner to create a thin sleeping bag, but it seems doubtful if any crews used this feature. It had a removable hood and numerous pockets, with a distinctive multiple pencil pocket on the breast of all suits. Inside there were braces so the top half could be shed back during hot work.

The last type of tank suit made during the war was called the Jungle Tank Suit, which was made of mosquito-proof tight weave cotton and included a rear 'trapdoor' for use at latrines. It does not appear to have been issued before the conflict ended. The Winter Suit continued to be made after the war and was issued for the next three decades. A number of countries copied the Tank Suit incorporating their own small variations.

#037 E2023.99

BLUEPRINT TRACING

Mavis Jones was one of the 'millions like us' women who worked in factories across Britain – in her case at Newton, Chambers in Sheffield building Churchill tanks.

A wartime marriage: Eddie and Mavis Jones on their wedding day in 1944.

'It was standing all the time at a drawing board but I enjoyed the work. I just had the T square and set squares, my drawings and a wooden step to stand on to reach the top. I liked the neatness of it all – you could see what you'd done at the end of the day.'

Most of Mavis's time was spent in the offices and she had little opportunity to visit the factory floor, but when she could, she liked to see the Churchills rolling off the assembly line and heading out onto the road. Despite the hard work, Mavis enjoyed her job at the factory and was able to find time for fun and relaxation. She met her husband, Lieutenant Eddie Jones, in 1943 when his unit encamped at the bottom of her garden. Within three weeks they were engaged and shortly after their marriage, Eddie was leading his men up Sword Beach on 6 June 1944.

'On D-Day I cried on my bicycle into work. I cried all day.'

Churchill tanks from the Newton, Chambers factory Mavis worked on may well have been on Sword Beach at the same time as her new husband landed with his men.

Eddie survived the war to return to Mavis and in 2016 she was invited to open The Tank Museum's Tank Factory Exhibition with HRH the Duke of Kent. Her blueprint was displayed in the mock-up of a drawing office.

Mavis Jones joined Newton, Chambers & Co as a 16-year-old in 1942. The Sheffield factory was a large employer in the area and manufactured Churchill tanks during the war. Mavis traced technical drawings using black ink on waxed linen.

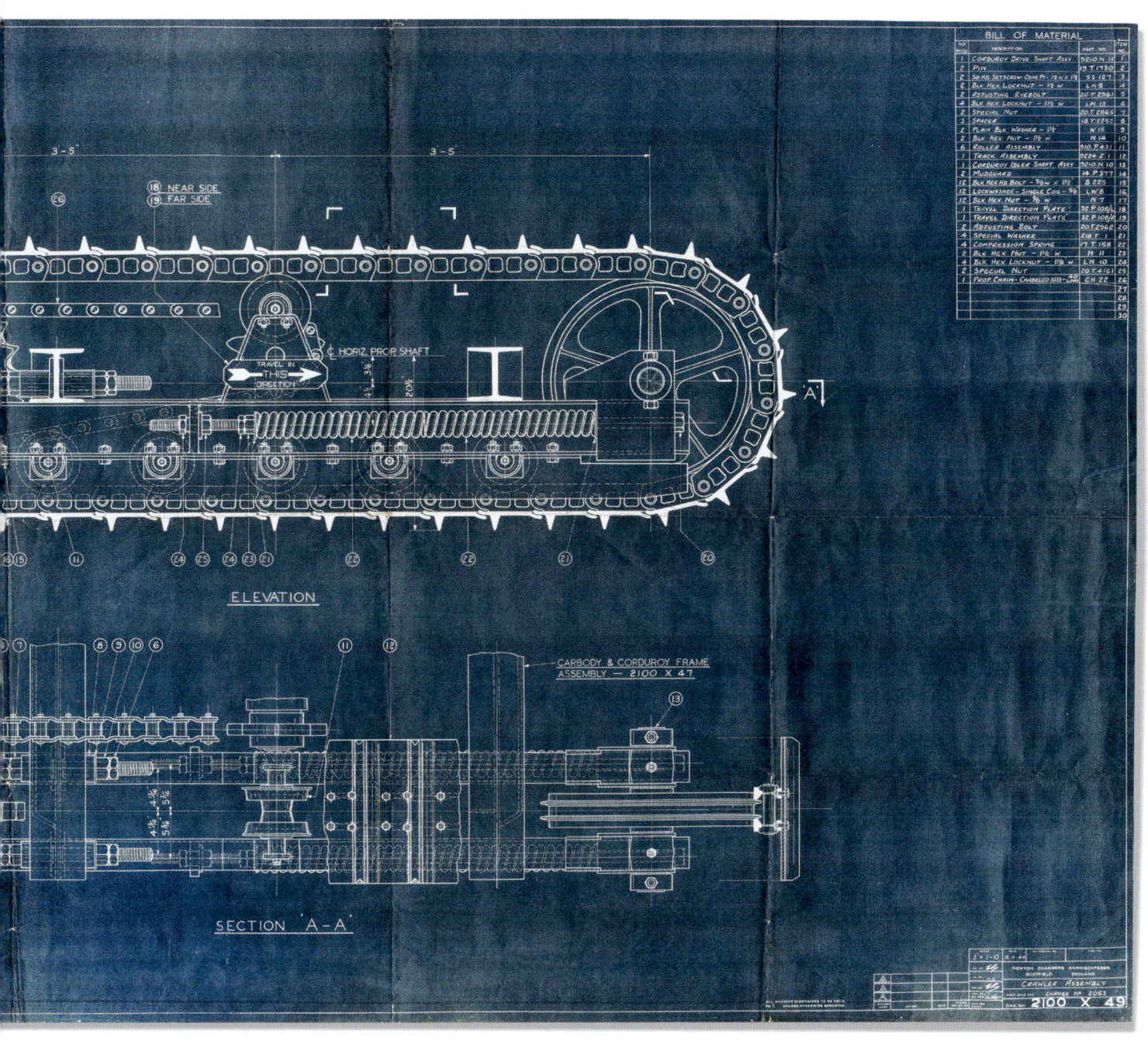

A drawing for crawler track copied by Mavis Jones. Her initials 'M.J.' can be seen in the bottom righthand corner.

The simple design of the PIAT belied its potency in use. Its main component was a cylindrical steel tube containing a powerful spring, at the end of which was a spigot and a trough into which was placed a hollow charge or high-explosive anti-tank projectile. This was fired by pulling a large trigger.

#038 E1992.160

PIAT
PROJECTOR, INFANTRY, ANTI-TANK

Crude and alarming to use though the PIAT was – it could do the job it was intended for. Here are the remains of a Panzer III knocked out by one in Italy.

The cumbersome PIAT was among the most effective infantry anti-tank weapons of its day, with six Victoria Crosses awarded to PIAT users in the Second World War.

Britain started the war with the Boys Anti-tank Rifle and a grenade that could be fired from a cup container on a rifle as their anti-tank weapons for the common infantryman. Both proved ineffective in service so new designs were sought.

Lieutenant Colonel Latham Valentine Stewart Blacker had a *Boys Own* career, serving on the North West Frontier, in the Royal Flying Corps in the First World War, and carrying out such daring exploits as flying over Mount Everest. He set himself up as a weapons designer and helped create a spigot weapon called the Blacker Bombard that some units of the Home Guard were issued with in 1940. Another of his designs – the Baby Bombard – was further developed by Major Millis Jefferis who worked at a unit called MD1 making weapons for a range of roles, but primarily for undercover work.

Using hollow charge ammunition, Jefferis rebuilt the Baby Bombard and had it test-fired at Bisley. The first firer was injured from metal flying back from the target, leading Jefferis to take over

of faults but was put into production in August 1942 and was first used in Tunisia in 1943. By the Normandy campaign the following year each platoon of infantry would have a PIAT with a two-man team – a firer and a loader.

The weapon had to be cocked by the user standing up and pulling on a strong spring. A bomb was then placed in the tray. A spigot or metal tube was released by pulling the trigger mechanism and this sprung forward setting off a charge in the hollow tube of the bomb's tail, causing it to fly out of the tray as far as 115yds (105m). Firing re-cocked the weapon.

Early failures with the bombs (a quarter failed to explode when hitting the target) were rectified but it was never made perfect. The weapon was heavy to carry but it did work and could penetrate 100mm (4in) of armour. It also had no back blast meaning it could be fired inside a building and had no smoke to reveal the firer's position. It could also be used against buildings and bunkers. Six Victoria Crosses were awarded

#039 E2005.361
LETTER HOME
NORMAN AGER

Letters home from a Royal Tank Regiment trooper to his mother included flora he had collected from the desert after the rains.

Pressed flora contained in one of Norman Ager's letters home to his mother at Harrow in North London.

Norman Ager of the 5th Royal Tank Regiment regularly wrote home to his mother, sometimes about the progress of the war, but more often about the horticulture he found on his wartime travels.

Serving in North Africa he wrote letter No 164 to his mother in March 1943. It began:

My dear mum,
With this short letter you will find or found a few flowers from the desert which I have pressed, but I am afraid not very good. I picked them at various places on my way up to Tripoli and they are a few of the great variety one sees at this time of the year after the rains.'

In other letters Norman sent his mother envelopes containing seeds, olive tree leaves, 'plants from the foot of the Great Pyramid' and an envelope containing 'Flowers from one of the many bunches and bouquets thrown on our tank in Ghent'.

Ager's mother saved his letters and he himself brought back and labelled many items and mementoes from his wartime experiences. These were donated by his family in 1994 along with his letters. Though small items, many reflect a poignant story. His tin of morphine capsules from a first aid kit had one of the glass capsules missing. In its place was a note from Ager saying, 'I used this on a wounded German soldier at El Alamein. I hope he made it.'

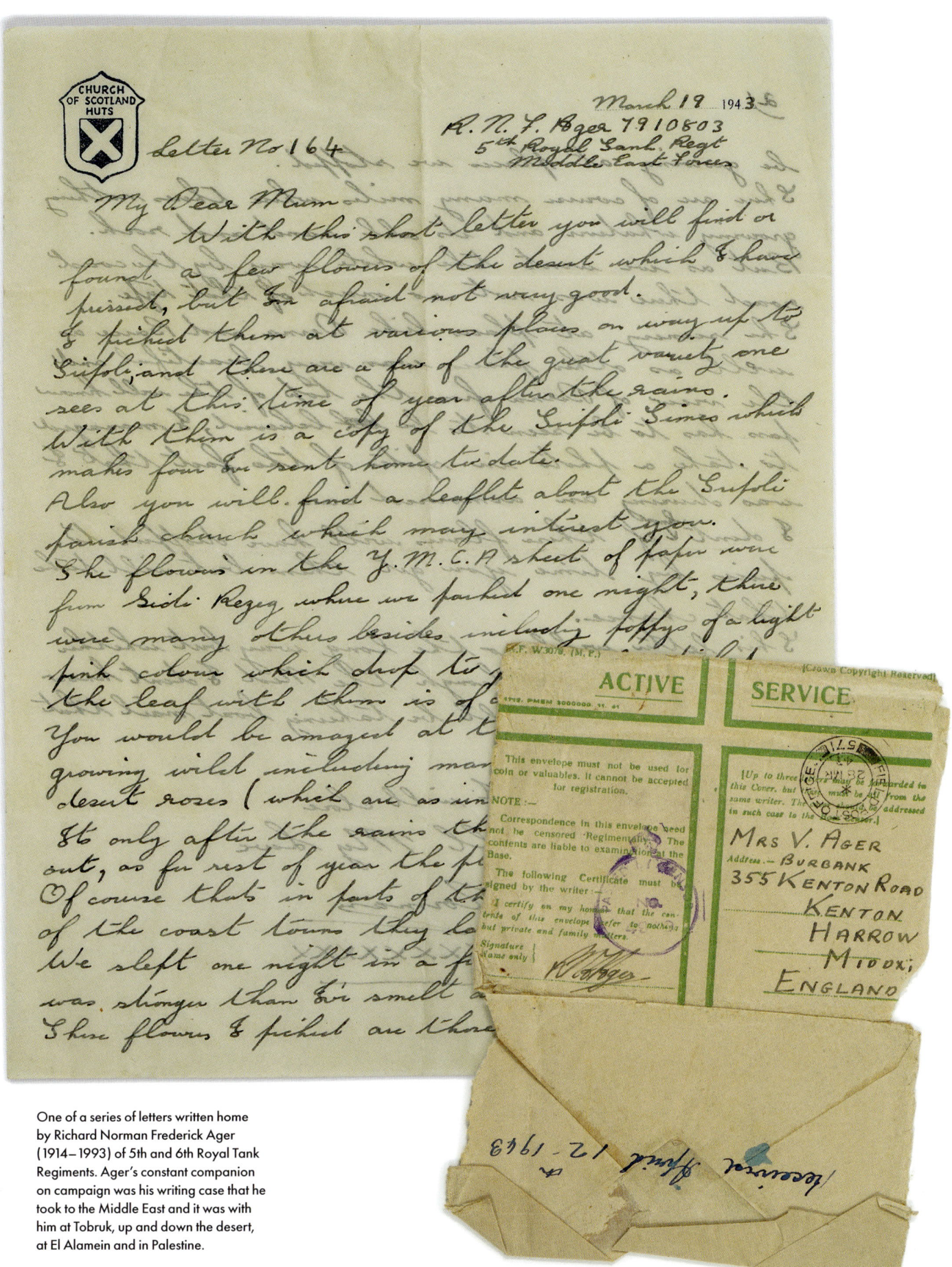

One of a series of letters written home by Richard Norman Frederick Ager (1914–1993) of 5th and 6th Royal Tank Regiments. Ager's constant companion on campaign was his writing case that he took to the Middle East and it was with him at Tobruk, up and down the desert, at El Alamein and in Palestine.

#040 E1994.130
MY SON JOHN
LEONARD JOHN FULLER ROI, RCA (1891–1973)

Artist Leonard John Fuller's portrait of his son John may owe something to his own service experience on the Western Front in the First World War.

Leonard Fuller served in France with the 10th Battalion Royal Fusiliers (in whose uniform he is seen here) and later the Machine Gun Corps. (Private Collection, courtesy Penlee House Gallery & Museum, Penzance)

Leonard Fuller studied at the Royal Academy Schools in London before he headed to the Western Front to serve with the Machine Gun Corps in the First World War. He returned to study art at the Royal Academy again after the war and went on to teach in a number of London schools and art colleges. He married fellow artist Marjorie Mostyn and together they moved to St Ives and established the St Ives School of Painting. In many ways he was a traditional artist, but Fuller was a major enthusiast of a number of more modern artists and helped create the St Ives School, where such prominent names as Ben Nicholson and his wife the scupltor Barbara Hepworth arrived in 1939 and settled there.

Fuller painted his son John as a three-quarter length portrait, in his greatcoat, collar up against the weather, gas mask slung over shoulder and pipe in hand. In the background a stylised tank can be seen against the thunderous sky.

John Fuller joined the Army in 1940 and was posted to 5th Royal Tank Regiment. He survived the war, leaving with the rank of sergeant.

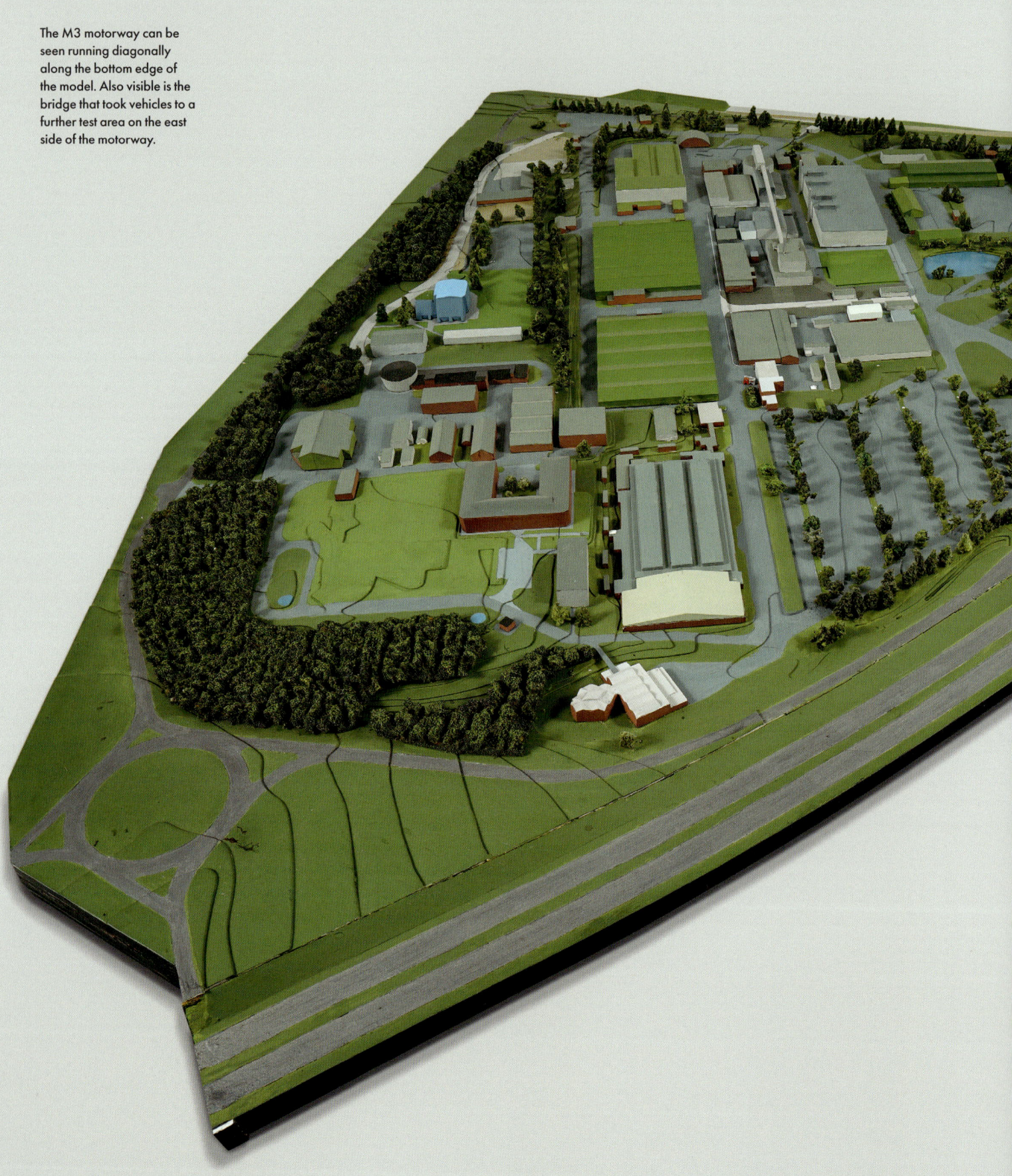

The M3 motorway can be seen running diagonally along the bottom edge of the model. Also visible is the bridge that took vehicles to a further test area on the east side of the motorway.

#041 E2015.516

SCALE MODEL OF THE RARDE SITE AT CHERTSEY

Enemy spies would have been justified in their confusion at the multiplicity of names used by the tank design and testing site at Chertsey.

This large model at 1:1000 scale shows the Royal Armament Research and Development Establishment (RARDE) based at Chertsey in Surrey. Vehicles and subcomponents were not just designed here, but they also could be tested. A modelling workshop helped produce a range of items to assist in this process. Here we can see a product of the workshop showing buildings in the 1980s, some of which were paid for by the Shah of Iran as part of his huge tank order. Buildings (some now listed) could be be used to test temperature, others to allow turrets to be slewed at angles and aimed at fixed points.

The development and testing of tanks in Britain took place in a number of locations, leading to a complex history of acronyms as bodies came and went or were renamed. The original design department at Woolwich Arsenal closed in 1923 with the idea that industry (mainly Vickers) would take over designing tanks. A testing body, the Tank and Tracked Transport Experiment Establishment (TTTEE) was formed at Farnborough in 1925, which was renamed the Mechanical Warfare Experimental Establishment (MWEE) in 1928. This in turn became the Mechanisation Experimental Establishment (MEE) in 1934 and it merged with parts of the Woolwich Design Department in 1940 to create the Department of Tank Design (DTD).

In 1942, the Department created a new wing at Chertsey on the former RAF Chobham site. This was called the Fighting Vehicles Proving Establishment (FVPE) and the following year the Wheeled Vehicles Experimental Establishment (WVEE) was also established on the site. The surrounding lowland heath of Chobham Common allowed vehicles to be test-driven. In written accounts there is a confusing number of names for the site, Chertsey, Chobham and even 'The Tank Factory'.

In the post-war period, amalgamations of various Government agencies led to seven more name changes for AFV design. The Chertsey site was sold in 2003 and currently forms part of what is known as Longcross Film Studios. The Tank Museum's Mark IV replica tank was made on the site for the film *War Horse*, which was released in 2011.

THE TANK MUSEUM IN 100 OBJECTS 87

#042 E2004.2477 & E2004.2461.1
THE COST

Among the thousands of letters and diaries from tank soldiers in The Tank Museum Archive there are many that tell stories of loss and sadness.

Corporal Charles Callwood, 144th Regiment, Royal Armoured Corps.

The museum holds many sets of Royal Armoured Corps medals awarded to recognise military service by a grateful nation. It also has thousands of letters and diaries from the soldiers. One particular group reveals something of the impact the conflict had on the Callwood family.

Corporal Charles Callwood was killed by a mortar bomb splinter as he sheltered under his tank on 12 August 1944 near Saint-Sylvain in Normandy. He was 31. In his wallet was a photograph (opposite) of his new baby daughter Joan.

The picture was returned to his wife, Amy, in Cheshire along with a series of letters from fellow crew members, his Troop Leader Lieutenant Marcus Cunliffe, and the Commanding Officer of his regiment, 144 Royal Armoured Corps, Lieutenant Colonel Alan Jolly DSO. All wanted her to know how respected and missed Charles was, and how they would do anything to help or assist her if they could. Lieutenant Cunliffe wrote to tell Mrs Callwood how the Padré found his grave 'is being well tended. It has a good cross, and there are flowers upon it, provided by the civilians. When he saw it, it was covered in dahlias, which the French are very fond of.'

Joan grew up knowing little about her father. Whenever his name was brought up her mother changed the subject or stopped the conversation, leading Joan to think her mother wanted to forget him. In the 1960s, Joan made the effort to visit France and her father's grave. After a traumatic trip on the ferry (Joan was frightened of water) and not being able to speak French (which meant initially she caught the wrong bus), Joan finally reached Bretteville-sur-Laize Cemetery. Finding his grave, Joan recalled, was 'very emotional as it had my name on it'. The inscription read: 'In memory's garden we meet every day. Loving wife and daughter Joan.'

Only then did Joan realise that her mother found the loss of her husband too painful to talk about. Her silence was not indifference, but a broken heart.

Joan gave these letters and her father's medals to The Tank Museum in 2004 and subsequently museum staff have been able to pay their respects at Charles Callwood's grave. One story in a cemetery of 2,958 stories.

Charles Callwood's medal group: the 1939–1945 Star, France and Germany Star, Defence Medal, and 1939–1945 War Medal.

Lieut. M F Cunliffe
HQ Sqn
144 RAC
BLA

22 Sep 44

Dear Mrs Callwood

Thank you for your letter.
I would have written to you before now to tell you about your husband's grave, but — as you'll understand — we have been on the move since he was killed, & only now has it been possible for us to find out exactly where he is buried. The Padre has been back to his grave & has told me all about it.

Your husband is buried in the 51st Highland Division cemetery near a big factory at CORMEILLES, which is a suburb to the south of CAEN (I print the names so that you are not misled by my bad writing). CAEN itself is of course badly smashed up, but the area round is not too bad. The Padre tells me [that the grave] is being well-tended. It has a [cross &] there are flowers upon it, provided [by the French]. When he saw it it was covered [with flowers] which the French are very fond of [...].

Your husband was killed in [...]

Above: Corporal Charles Callwood's grave at Bretteville-sur-Laize Cemetery in Normandy.

Left: A letter from Charles Callwood's Troop Leader, Lieutenant Marcus Cunliffe, to his widow, Amy.

Bottom: The commanding officer of 144th Regiment, RAC, Lieutenant Colonel Alan Jolly, wrote a letter of condolence to Charles's widow. Jolly had been commissioned into the Royal Tank Corps in 1931 and later rose to become Quartermaster-General in 1966.

From:-
No. 49887 Lt. Col. A. Jolly, D.S.O.
Commanding 144th Regt. RAC
B.L.A.

28th Sept. 1944.

Dear Mrs Callwood.

I am glad to be able at last to write you a few lines to express my sympathy with you in your great loss. As you probably realise, we have been almost continuously in action & it has not been possible for me to do this until now.

I know that no words of mine can be of much comfort to you but it may perhaps be of some little help to realise what an important part was played in the recent victories by this Regiment, which your husband served so well. I have had a letter from the RAC General at Field Marshal Montgomery's headquarters in which he says how well the 144 has done. & though this cannot compensate you for the loss of your

Love never dies: a short but tender message from Joan's father, Charles.

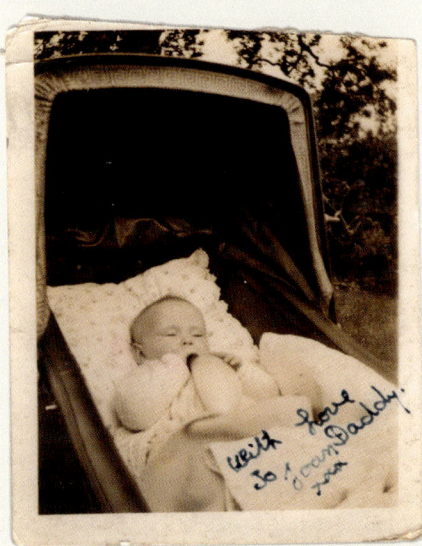

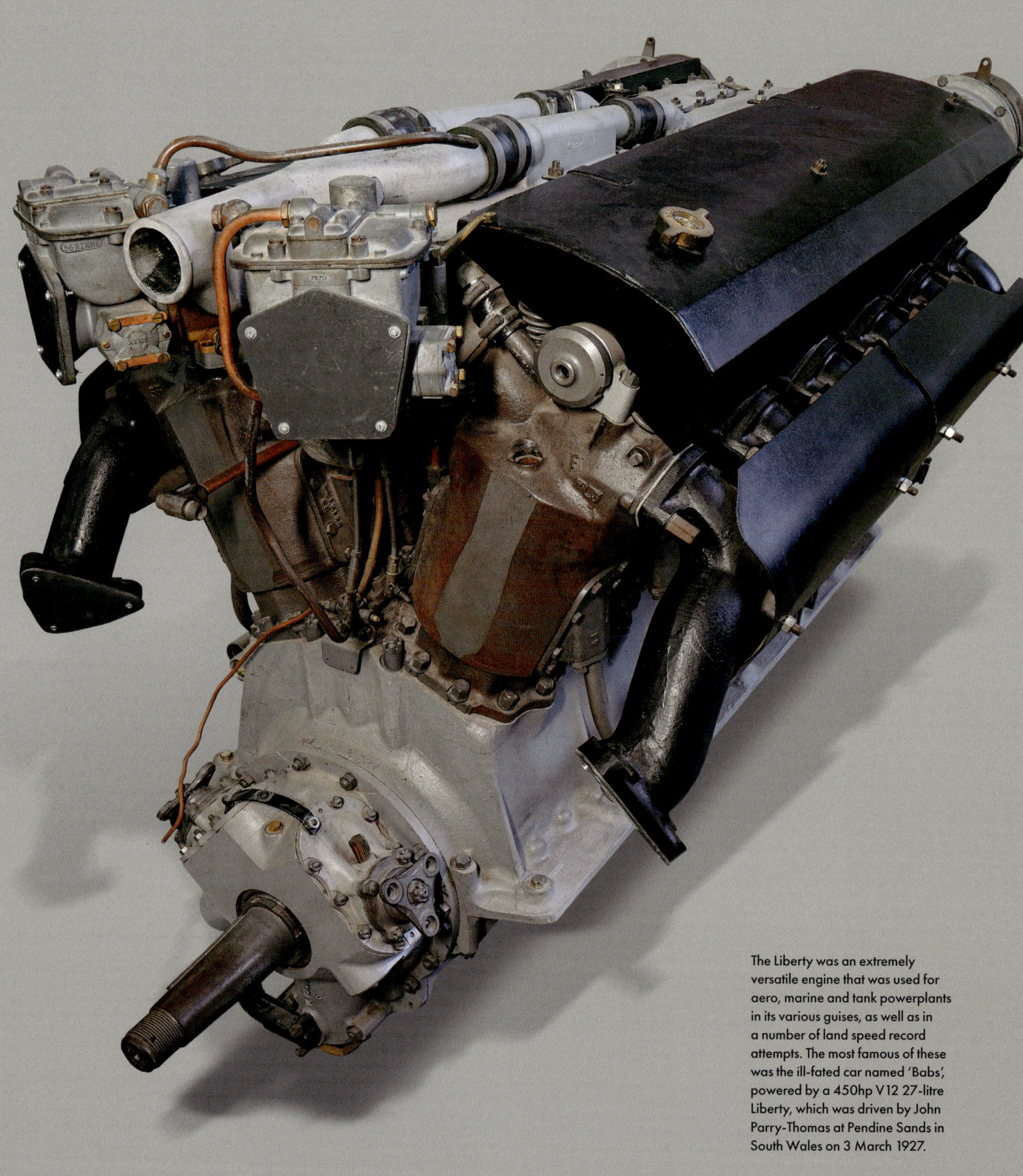

The Liberty was an extremely versatile engine that was used for aero, marine and tank powerplants in its various guises, as well as in a number of land speed record attempts. The most famous of these was the ill-fated car named 'Babs', powered by a 450hp V12 27-litre Liberty, which was driven by John Parry-Thomas at Pendine Sands in South Wales on 3 March 1927.

#043 E1955.38
LIBERTY ENGINE

The US needed a standard design that could be quickly mass-produced, so only proven components were used to ensure a workable engine in the shortest timeframe.

Designed originally as an aero engine, the Liberty powerplant was used in tanks for more than 20 years. In May 1917, the US Aircraft Production Board invited Jesse Vincent and Elbert Hall, who were two top automotive engineers, to design a new engine with a high power-to-weight ratio that could be quickly mass-produced. After five days in a Washington hotel room they emerged with a new design and by July a prototype 8-cylinder version had been built, with a 12-cylinder version becoming available in August.

The engine's modular design allowed cylinders to be banked together, creating V8 or V12 models, and an order for 22,500 engines was placed with six automobile manufacturers. A new feature of production saw parts being specially manufactured and distributed to assembly sites. Ford made all the cylinders, over 2,000 a day, by devising new production techniques.

Design of the 'International' or Mark VIII tank was a joint project between the US, Britain and France. A version of the V12 engine with cast iron cylinders was produced for the American-built tanks. The engine created 300hp, but the 100 tanks built in the USA were too late to see action in the First World War.

A version of the Liberty was used by Soviet Russia for their BT (or fast) series of tanks. These were inspired by a Liberty-powered tank designed by the American Walter Christie. In Britain the

Liberty engines being fitted into the engine bays of British Crusader I tanks.

Nuffield Organisation redesigned a Liberty engine to become the powerplant for the Cruiser Mark III (the A13 Mk 1). Built in Britain, the first engines had 340hp, but after eight major variant changes during the production run the engine was made to produce 410hp. Liberty engines were fitted to five variants of Cruiser tanks, the last being the Cavalier and Centaur, designed as part of the Cromwell family. The 600hp Rolls-Royce Meteor engine then became available and was used for British tanks until the 1960s.

#044 E1986.121
SHERMAN V
THEODORE CHARLES BASIL HITCHCOCK (1892–1953)

Hitchcock's depiction in oils of a Sherman V of the Westminster Dragoons climbing a bank shows a keen eye for detail and a sense of the tank in motion.

Hitchcock was an artist and teacher, having studied at Hornsey School of Art. Here one of his teachers was Adrian Hill who had been an Official War Artist in the First World War; another was John Charles Moody, who painted traditional architectural views and promoted art as a therapy. He regularly exhibited at the Royal Academy and other London venues in a fluid, impressionistic style.

This painting of a tank – an M4A4 Sherman V climbing a bank – shows a real facility with the oil paint medium. The background as to how the painting of this picture came about is not currently known, which is disappointing as the image seems to be of a real place and event, not just a stylised imagined view of a Sherman tank.

The Sherman V was the British name for what the US military called the M4A4 model that housed the Chrysler multibank engine. The US had hoped to use the Wright Continental air-cooled engine in the Sherman, but this was also an engine needed by the expanding aircraft industry, so alternatives were sought. Chrysler came up with the idea of bolting five six-cylinder car engines onto a common drive shaft. This engine required the hull to be lengthened by 11 in and in consequence the suspension units are more spread out. The tank became the heaviest mass-produced model of Sherman, but it had the lowest ground pressure due to the lengthening of the tracks.

The US Army used few M4A4s and only for training, but Britain received 7,167 of the 7,499 made and thought them reliable, converting a number into the Firefly, or Sherman VC.

A Sherman V of the Westminster Dragoons in the North West Europe Campaign.

It is almost possible to imagine the bellow of the Chrysler multibank engine as the driver of this Sherman V positions his tank to climb the earthen bank depicted in this oil on board painting. Sadly, Hitchcock was not to make old bones and was drowned in a sailing accident in 1953.

#045 E2015.3723

BLOWN 2-POUNDER BARREL

This graphic example of gun barrel failure could have happened for any number of reasons.

Items such as this split 2pdr gun barrel were kept to show troops as part of teaching collections. Needless to say, there are a number of reasons that might cause a gun barrel to fail.

For barrels that fired high explosive rounds a 'premature' meant the round exploded inside the barrel. Gun barrels are designed to take huge pressures but not the force of an explosive round detonating inside them.

'Plugging' means something jamming inside the barrel to block it – for a tank gun this could be mud or soil. Long guns, facing forward could bury themselves in the ground as the tank travelled over rough terrain. Crews were taught to reverse the turret or turn the gun to the side to stop this happening. The firing of a plugged gun could mean the round simply cannot progress out of the barrel and the force built up behind the projectile either causes the breach to fail or the barrel to split to release the pressure.

Gun barrels have been tested or 'proofed' for centuries and stamped accordingly that they made the grade. If a failure did occur it was important to know the reason why: were sub-standard materials used, or was a manufacturing process not completed to the right standard?

During combat, guns could also get damaged by shell splinters, or by strikes from other incoming projectiles. If the gun cannot take the pressure it was designed to take – such as from becoming worn due to overuse – it could fail again. Because of this the number of rounds fired was recorded for each gun, the type of round fired (some types wear the barrel out faster than others), and checks on the barrel carried out regularly to determine whether it was serviceable or if it needed replacing.

The failure of a barrel meant the tank could not perform its key function, and there was also the real danger of injury to a crewmember or even the possibility of a fatality.

Above: A catastrophic failure of a 2pdr gun barrel.

Right: A 2pdr barrel on a Matilda II in the Western Desert that has suffered a catastrophic failure.

#046 E1992.205

PANZERFAUST

The Germans made more than eight million Panzerfaust single-use hollow charge anti-tank weapons before the end of the Second World War.

This simple anti-tank weapon saw widespread use from 1943 onwards by the German Army. The 'tank' or 'armour fist' was launched by a single soldier, holding the launch tube under his arm and blasting the warhead forward – depending on the model – to 30, 60, 100 or 150m. The tube that had contained the black powder propellant could then be thrown away. A wooden shaft behind the warhead carried folded, stabilising fins, which sprung out to keep the warhead on a straight flightpath. The hollow charge warhead could penetrate around 200mm of armour plate, which was more than that carried by most Allied tanks. It is estimated that over eight million Panzerfausts of all types were made before the end of the Second World War.

The phenomenon of the 'hollow charge' had been known about since the end of the 19th century. An explosive charge with a wedge shape or hollow cut into its face, when placed against a piece of armour plate, caused greater penetration. It was known as the 'Monroe' or 'Neumann' effect. Improvements such as the cutting of a wedge shape, detonating the charge away from the surface (the 'stand-off'), and lining the inner wedge or cone of explosive with a malleable metal, all increased the depth of armour that could be penetrated.

Detonation of the hollow charge caused the metal liner (usually copper) to break up and form into a metal jet and plug, which then penetrated the armoured target. The metal jet sped forward at 8–9,000m/sec and by its sheer kinetic energy (around 200 tons/sq in) it pushed the armour plate out of the way creating a small hole. The general rule was that a warhead could penetrate metal depth about three or four times the diameter of the cone. Having penetrated the armour plate, the jet could cause spalling (pieces of metal flying off inside the armoured hull), fires from the hot jet, or injury to the crew.

The Panzerfaust's availability in huge numbers meant it was issued widely as a simple to use defensive weapon for German forces as they retreated. In Germany, Hitler Youth and Volkssturm (or Home Guard) units were sent out on bicycles armed with the weapon to ambush advancing Allied tanks in a last-ditch home defence.

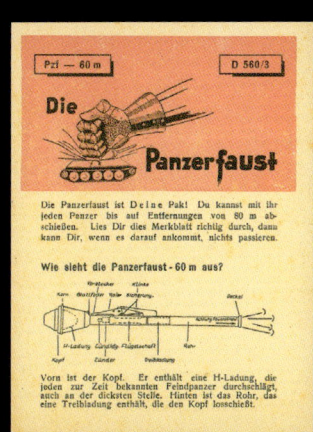

The instruction pamphlet issued with the Panzerfaust.

#047 E1985.121

RAM KANGAROO

Designed and built by Canada, the Ram Kangaroo was a successful adaptation of the Ram tank based on the American M3 Medium tank chassis.

The principle of carrying infantry forward under some form of armoured protection had been tried before the end of First World War. Tanks led the infantry and allowed them to advance, but it was easy for them to be held up or lose contact with each other. The Mark IX tank was based on the Mark V but made longer to carry 30 soldiers internally. Conditions for the soldiers inside the vehicle caused disorientation and nausea, but only three vehicles were completed by 1918 and they did not see action.

During the Second World War, in the close wooded country of Normandy, good armour and infantry cooperation was paramount – the two arms needed to support each other. The use of half-tracks and carriers provided a way of bringing some infantry forward to keep up with tanks, but there were not enough and the commander of the II Canadian Corps, Lieutenant General Guy Simmonds, came up with an idea. The Canadians had new artillery in the form of Sexton self-propelled guns and towed 25pdr guns, meaning they had 72 redundant 105mm-armed M7 Priest self-propelled guns. As part of 'Project Kangaroo', Simmonds had the Priest's guns removed and the front housing plated over in field workshops. The vehicles were first used operationally in August 1944 and their success led to 500 Ram tanks being converted into Ram Kangaroos. Other vehicles such as the Churchill and Sherman were also used.

The Ram tanks had their turrets removed, climbing aids added for the 8–10 infantry passengers, and stowage arrangements were changed. By December 1944, the 1st Canadian Armoured Carrier Regiment had been formed as part of the 79th Armoured Division, later joined by a similar British formation, the 49th Armoured Personnel Carrier Regiment.

In his memoir *A Full Life*, Lieutenant General Brian Horrocks, Commander of XXX Corps, wrote of the Kangaroos that they 'proved a great boon in the closing stages of the war... I once saw a whole brigade of the 51st Highland Division in these vehicles being heavily shelled by the Germans. I thought their casualties were bound to be high, but they had only two men wounded.'

Ram Kangaroo *Brighton II* passes an abandoned German Flak gun in 1945.

THE TANK MUSEUM IN 100 OBJECTS 99

#048 E1951.49

TOG II*

Designed for a First World War battlefield, the British TOG II* was of no use in the more mobile Second World War.

A new Special Vehicle Development Committee was set up in 1939, aiming to bring together the people who had been instrumental in inventing the tank during the First World War, and coming up with ideas for a new armoured vehicle.

Sir Albert Stern led the group, which included Sir Eustace Tennyson d'Eyncourt, Sir Ernest Swinton, Harry Ricardo and Walter Gordon Wilson. Inevitably, the group acquired the nickname 'the old gang', hence 'TOG'. They visited France and tried to ascertain the likely problems the British Army would face. Believing warfare may again mean trenches and a heavily shelled zone of battle, the committee came up with a heavy tank design. This was given

TOG II was an improved version of the first TOG iteration, while TOG II* seen here was a further modification with the turret of the A30 Challenger tank and a 3.7in gun.

to William Tritton at Fosters in Lincoln to build. The tank was to have sponsons to mount 2pdr guns and a field gun in the front. An electric drive system was used – the engine ran two generators with an electric motor for each track. For the first trials a turret from a Matilda II tank was placed on top, and a 75mm hull gun from a French Char B tank in the front hull, but side sponsons were not fitted.

Changes to the drive system and waning interest from the War Office saw the project drag on. A second model was developed, now with tracks that ran lower beneath the side doors instead of around the frame (as in a First World War tank). A new and more effective electric drive system was used and the vehicle first ran in March 1941.

Improvements were made – a version of the new turret for the A30 Challenger tank was fitted and torsion bar suspension was trialled in May 1943. Despite the huge size of the vehicle and weight of 80 tons, contemporary film shows it to be much more manoeuvrable than might be imagined. TOG I was probably scrapped, TOG II survived and became part of The Tank Museum collection. It remained outside for many years – the hall in which it is housed, the Tamiya Hall, was built over it.

Apart from its sheer size and the story of being one of the odder wartime British developments, few showed any interest in TOG. However, since its involvement in an online computer game the tank has attracted a large following.

#049 E2008.3085.2

BRIXMIS SOUVENIR SIGN

Enamel signs like this one were intended to warn off patrols by foreign military liaison missions in East Germany, but this example was 'souvenired' by a BRIXMIS team.

To know the capabilities of your enemy, or potential enemy, and what they have in the way of equipment has always been an issue for military forces. For tanks, details such as the thickness of the armour or the size of the tank gun are crucial facts to know. This is so your own capabilities can 'overmatch' the enemy threat – you need a gun capable of penetrating their armour and of course, in turn, levels of protection to defeat the projectiles fired at you.

To discover this information, how equipment might be used and by whom, various intelligence gathering agencies exist. In the Cold War, one such organisation used the cover of the British Commanders'-in-Chief Mission to the Soviet Forces in Germany – or BRIXMIS. Begun in 1946 in occupied Germany 'to maintain liaison between the Staff of the two Commanders-in-Chief and their Military Governments in the Zones', the Soviet and British militaries created teams of 31 members who were allowed access around the other's zones

Corporal Keith Marshall and Lieutenant Colonel Stephen Harrison MBE after stealing the 'Keep Out' sign.

TENTION! PASSAGE OF MEMBERS
F foreign MILITARY LIAISON
MISSIONS PROHIBITED!

ATTENTION! PASSAGE AUX
BRES des MISSIONS MILITAIRES
ANGERES de LIAISON est INTERDIT!

ОЕЗД ЧЛЕНАМ ИНОСТРАННЫХ
НЫХ МИССИЙ СВЯЗИ ЗАПРЕЩЕН!

rchfahrt für das Personal der
ändischen Militärverbindungs-
MISSIONEN ist VERBOTEN!

for liaison purposes. As the Cold War deepened the opportunity of using this agreement to gather intelligence became obvious to both sides.

Often shadowed by the East German State Security Service (the Stasi), a three-man BRIXMIS team would head off dressed in uniform, in marked but tuned-up vehicles to gather information. This would sometimes be in response to direct requests from Defence Intelligence based in London, but occasionally it was to take up random opportunities. They needed subterfuge and speed to lose those who were tracking them, and the Soviet authorities restricted certain areas to the prying eyes of BRIXMIS.

Military bases were sneaked into, parts were stolen, discarded rubbish was searched for paperwork, and bored Soviet guards were bribed with watches and pornography. Soviet bases warned off any approach with signs such as this, which became perfect souvenirs for the team members.

One notable BRIXMIS success occurred when a train carrying the latest Soviet BMP-2 armoured personnel carrier stopped at a level crossing in front of a team. A BRIXMIS member jumped the barrier and using an apple from his lunch box, stuffed it into the end of the barrel and was thus able to deduce the calibre of the new weapon.

The 'captured' sign bears its message in German as well as in the languages of the English, French and Soviet occupying powers in postwar Germany.

#050 E1955.32

SHERMAN TANK 'MICHAEL'

'Michael' was the first Lend-Lease Sherman tank and is now the oldest surviving example of a Sherman in the world.

'Michael' has two significant features not seen on later production Shermans. One is the main armament sight, set in the top of the turret; the other is the extra pair of machine-guns at the front, operated by the driver.

The US President Franklin D. Roosevelt had great sympathy for the British and French fight against fascism when war broke out in 1939. American public opinion, however, and American laws stemming from the post-First World War isolationist stance, along with Neutrality Acts in the 1930s, stopped any direct support for the Allied war effort. This position gradually changed, led by the President and the entry of America into the war after the Japanese attack on Pearl Harbor on 7 December 1941.

Britain set up a 'Purchasing Commission' firstly in Canada, then Washington, to help coordinate the acquisition of war materials. In November 1939, US laws were changed to allow foreign buyers of military material to purchase on a 'cash and carry' basis. This favoured Britain who, with its trading empire and relative wealth, could place orders and ship material across the Atlantic. Germany would be at a disadvantage with less foreign currency and a smaller shipping fleet. It would also have to avoid the Royal Navy (as no bought war material could be transported in US ships).

Orders were placed by the Purchasing Commission in the US for tank parts, then enquiries were made to see if entire tanks could be ordered and built. Britain was not alone in this purchasing spree. France, too, was placing orders with American manufacturers and Britain discussed a 50/50 split of the proposed Char B tank production.

'Michael' is unloaded on Horse Guards Parade in Central London where it was put on public display in 1942 as the first Sherman tank to be delivered to the UK under the Lend-Lease scheme.

The collapse of France weeks later in June 1940 ended the project and Britain began discussing ordering Matilda II and Crusader tanks from US companies. However, in late 1940, the US authorities were looking to increase their own tank production and suggested Britain buy into American designs that were to be built anyway, rather than commission their own.

The decision was quickly made to order American-designed tanks and information from the British experience of armoured warfare was fed to the US designers. Some 1,500 M3 Grant tanks were ordered and cash contracts also included orders for the forthcoming M4 Sherman tank: US$132 million worth of tank orders were placed by Britain and US$16 million was spent on building capacity, new factories and tooling. Just as Britain ran out of money in March 1941, Roosevelt was able to pass the Lend-Lease Act, allowing him to 'sell, transfer title to, exchange, lease, lend, or otherwise dispose of... any defence article'.

Michael Dewar was Chairman of the Birmingham-based company British Timken Ltd and had good contacts and a working knowledge of American industry, so he was placed in charge of the British Tank Mission in Washington. The Americans fitted a brass plate bearing the name 'Michael' on this Sherman M4A1 as a thank you for his efforts. 'Michael' was the second tank built in the Lima Locomotive Works in March 1942 under the early British production orders. It was rushed across the Atlantic, offloaded at Woolwich and then shown off on Horse Guards Parade in Central London on 8 May.

'Michael' is now the oldest Sherman remaining. It had some modifications in its wartime service, including replacing the original 75mm M2 gun and its counterweight with a new M3 gun.

#051 E2012.4782

STUART HAMILTON'S PHOTO ALBUM

Personal photograph albums can open windows onto the visceral experiences of fighting men.

Major Stuart Hamilton MC compiled two photograph albums that covered his time with the 8th Royal Tank Regiment in North Africa, Syria and Italy with the Eighth Army.

The Tank Museum has over 1,200 photographic albums in its Archive, and some contain outstanding images that capture servicemen in all facets of their military journey. Many reveal a journey from home life — the picture in the back garden with parents, a sister, the favourite pet, the first pictures in uniform, training, the formal official unit picture, girlfriend, deployment, postcards from abroad, the crew next to a vehicle, a family they were billeted with, a studio portrait from a day's leave and shots with mates called 'Alf', 'Chalkie' or 'Des'.

This album was put together by Stuart Hamilton of the 8th Royal Tank Regiment. It covers his time in North Africa and has some outstanding images of exhausted crews. Hamilton recalled in his memoir, *Armoured Odyssey*, 'we were all completely and utterly exhausted, both physically and mentally because we had been in continuous action for something like five weeks and we were walking like automatons'. The unit had been in action carrying out a fighting retreat to El Alamein in July 1942. There is one caption that perhaps sums up their experience: 'Self, Reggie [Campbell] and unknown replacement officer killed a day or two later... Very tired. Desert sores on nose, hands and legs.'

Stuart Hamilton enlisted as a trooper in the Royal Tank Corps in 1936, becoming an officer and a squadron leader in the Second World War.

In the digital age, few people print images and put them in the traditional-style albums, leaving them instead on hard drives or laptops. Although pictures are now taken in vast numbers, it is unlikely they will survive or be captioned for future study as laptops will fail, hard drives get corrupted and digital photographs lost. Archives are now starting to print digital media as a way of ensuring its survival.

THE TANK MUSEUM IN 100 OBJECTS 107

John Hassall opened his own New Art School and School of Poster Design in Kensington in 1900 where he numbered Bruce Bairnsfather, the humourist and cartoonist creator of 'Old Bill', among his students. His heyday was the Edwardian period when his theatrical posters covered the West End.

#052 E1970.56

A TANK IN ACTION
JOHN HASSALL (1868–1948)

John Hassall may have used 'Mother' as the model for his painting as there are features like the sponson apertures suggesting the tank is not a production Mark I.

John Hassall wanted to join the Army but failed his Sandhurst entrance exam. After a spell farming with his brother in Canada, he returned to Europe to draw for some illustrated magazines and to study art. He joined the company David Allen & Sons and started on a long career of designing posters. Probably his most famous work is the skipping jolly fisherman for the London and North Eastern Railway (LNER) poster – 'Skegness is SO bracing' (1908).

During the First World War, Hassall produced many posters in aid of the war effort or military charities, often for free. He also took on painting commissions and in 1917 William Foster & Co Ltd, builders of 'Little Willie' and 'Mother', asked Hassall to paint a tank picture. It is thought that 'Mother' was used as the model as there are some features, such as the sponson apertures, which indicate the tank is not a production Mark I. Hassall went to Fosters to make sketches and had a ride in a tank on the test area. His original painting was presented to the Usher Art Gallery in Lincoln when Fosters closed down. The Tank Museum has a third copy of the painting, but the whereabouts of the second is unknown.

John Hassall was an illustrator, designer, painter and teacher, as well as being a popular cartoonist and poster designer. (Chronicle /Alamy Stock Photo)

Solomon J. Solomon, the Royal Academician, had been approached to come up with a suitable paint scheme for tanks – he was already working on camouflage projects for the Army. Solomon saw 'Mother' at the Elveden training area in May 1916 and with six men, he painted a camouflage scheme on the tank. Lieutenant Basil Henriques saw Solomon at work and described the scheme: 'The effect was a kind of rather jolly landscape in green against a pink sunset sky'. 'Mother' was repainted, and by March 1917 she was in monotone, but an image exists of her wearing Solomon's scheme.

Hassall's painting for Fosters appears to show the Solomon scheme. Although all the crews had to paint their own tanks to mimic the scheme on 'Mother', by the time they went into action they had all been repainted by their crews. The overall pattern looked similar but the colour palate changed to try and blend with the Somme landscape.

Fosters used the painting in its advertising and sales literature, and colour prints of the picture were distributed.

#053 E1949.327

MARK V

9199 is a combat veteran that saw action towards the end of the First World War on the first day of the Battle of Amiens, 8 August 1918, when its commander won the Military Cross.

In July 1918, this Mark V tank was issued to the 8th Battalion Tank Corps. It has serial number 9199 (a number that would stay with the vehicle) and it was assigned to crew H41 (H being the eighth letter of the alphabet to correspond with the battalion number). Under the command of Lieutenant Harold Whittenbury, the eight men of H41 took 9199 into battle at 8.20am on 8 August 1918, the first day of the Battle of Amiens.

Whittenbury reported they 'Drove down steep slope into ravine... opened fire with both six pounders firing 6pdr (HE) and case shot at 40yds range into the trenches and dugouts. Also fired a good many rounds with front Hotchkiss and observed many casualties.'

At the end of the battle, the crew had fired 87 6pdr rounds, 18 case shots and 1,960 rounds from the Hotchkiss machine-guns. For his part in the action that day, Whittenbury was awarded the Military Cross.

H41 and 9199 were next in action on 23 August, commanded this time by Lieutenant Thomas Joseph DeCourcey. During the engagement a German machine-gun nest was captured. On 29 September, the tank, with an unknown crew, led the infantry in an attack on the village of Estrées. Lieutenant Thomas Roland Harding was in command and reported later that 'Fire seemed to be coming from all directions... fired on a light field gun position... my tank was hit near the left idler sprocket.' Harding was able to get back to the pre-arranged rallying point where his left track finally broke.

After the war tank 9199 was used for crew training before being issued in 1921 to the 4th Battalion Tank Corps based on Worgret Heath Camp not far from Bovington. By 1925, it had returned to Bovington Camp and was used for recovery work. The vehicle was donated to the museum collection in 1949 and appeared in a number of parades and events in running order. Before the 100th Anniversary commemorations of the First World War, The Tank Museum decided against running the vehicle as stress cracks were apparent in the metalwork. Repairs could have been made but in an attempt to preserve what original material remained the decision was made to retire the Mark V and obtain a replica to run instead.

Harold Whittenbury pictured as a private when he first joined the Army as one of the 'Manchester Pals'.

#054 E1972.243

FIRST MESSAGE TO A TANK IN ACTION

A flimsy note from the commander of a platoon of New Zealand troops requesting assistance is a priceless memento of the first ever tank attack.

On 15 September 1916, the first tank attack took place at Flers-Courcelette. The tanks were spread across the attack front, four tanks from D Company were tasked to support the 2nd Battalion of the 3rd New Zealand Rifle Brigade. At 9.15am, Lieutenant Charles Edward Butcher of the 2nd Battalion tasked Rifleman Joseph William Dobson to take a message to a tank they saw nearby.

'To O/C "Tanks" Enemy Machine Guns appear to be holding up infantry in valley on your right. Can you assist in pushing forward.

'C.E. Butcher, Lieut, Commanding
15 Platoon, Reserve Company, 2/3
N.Z.(R) B. 15/9/16 9.15a.m.'

Dobson recalled in 1973, running from 'shell hole to shell hole'. He said, 'They had a pop at me once and I got into a shell hole and then got going again. I got inside the tank and guided to where these machine guns were, in a far building and the tank just pushed it over. Germans scattered in all directions.'

Lieutenant Butcher later wrote of the tank – D12, commanded by Captain Graeme Nixon – 'Its

This is tank D7, which got stuck on 15 September. D12, the recipient of this message, suffered a worse fate. It was hit, set on fire and burnt out. Gunner William Debenham was killed.

destruction of the machine gun nest enabled two full-strength companies to advance rapidly and consolidate our objectives, which had been won at terrific cost by our two leading companies.'

Butcher was wounded later on 15 September, which led to the amputation of his right arm; Dobson was wounded at the Battle of Messines but returned to New Zealand and retained this message – almost certainly the first ever communication to a tank in action.

This is the brief message written in pencil on grid paper that was carried by a New Zealand rifleman across the battlefield at Flers-Courcelette to a tank of D Company requesting its help in destroying an enemy machine-gun position. That it was retained by the soldier, surviving the war and enduring for more than a century before its donation to The Tank Museum is a minor miracle.

From Lieut. BUTCHER
To O.C. "Tanks"

Enemy Machine Guns appear to be holding up infantry in valley on your right.

Can you assist in pushing forward.

C C Butcher
Lieut.
Commanding 15 Platoon
Reserve Company
2/3 NZRB

15/9/16
9:15 AM

#055 E1983.201

ARMOURED BARREL MG 34

The recoil-operated air-cooled general-purpose MG 34 was the backbone of the German Army's support weapons throughout the Second World War.

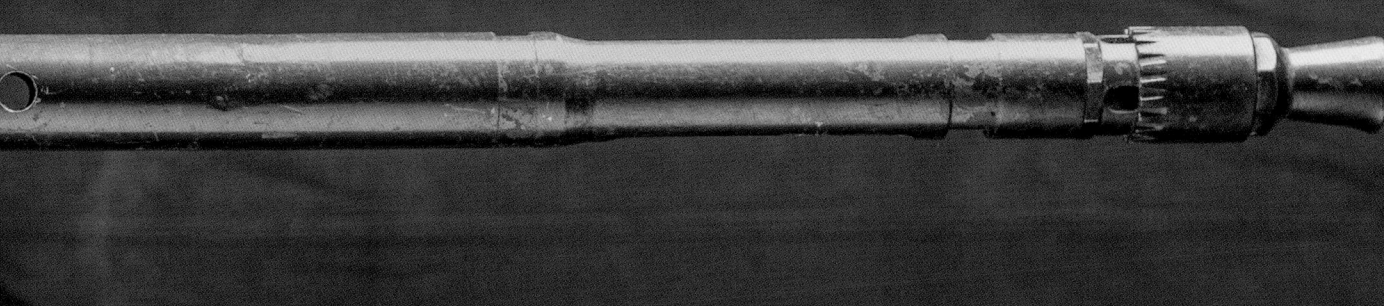

The MG 34 machine-gun is considered to be the first general purpose machine-gun. Designed to replace a number of guns used in specific roles, it had a fast rate of fire (needed if used against fleeting aircraft targets) and a quick-change barrel so it did not overheat in a sustained fire role.

A variety of mounts were designed to house the gun in the different roles for which it would be used. It was light enough for one man to carry and use.

For armoured vehicles, used as the secondary armament, the MG 34 replaced the earlier MG 13. The *Kugelblende* or ball-mount was fitted to a range of German armoured vehicles to house the MG 34. It was made in three models – 30, 50, or 80 – as a reference to the thickness of the armour used. The gun could be angled 15 degrees left or right of centre, and plus 20 or minus 10 degrees up or down. A small angled sight, the *Kugelzielfernrohr (KZf) 2*, could be fitted, but the expectation was the gun would be used out to a range of 200m. Aiming from inside a tank, especially when moving, would be very difficult.

Exposed outside the tank, the machine-gun barrel was susceptible to damage from small-arms fire and shell splinters. This led to the

An MG-34 fitted as a co-axial mount alongside the main gun. In this configuration it was aimed using the same sight as the main gun and usually fired by a foot pedal.

introduction of the *Panzermantel für MG 34* or an armoured barrel housing, officially accepted for service on 2 February 1941. It is estimated that over 50,000 of these armoured barrels were made during the war – far more than the vehicles to fit them to. The gun could be removed from the vehicle and a bipod mount was carried in the tank in a box also containing a sling, wooden butt and anti-aircraft sight.

The *Gurtsack* was also specially designed for vehicle use; a canvas bag to contain 150 of the 7.92mm rounds on a metal belt. These canvas bags were hung from metal strips inside the vehicle within easy reach of the crew.

#056 E2017.1979
WARTIME SKETCHBOOK
WILLIAM 'BILL' HEWISON (1925–2002)

Bill Hewison's life saw him progress from art student to tank soldier and back again to his first love as a cartoonist for *Punch*.

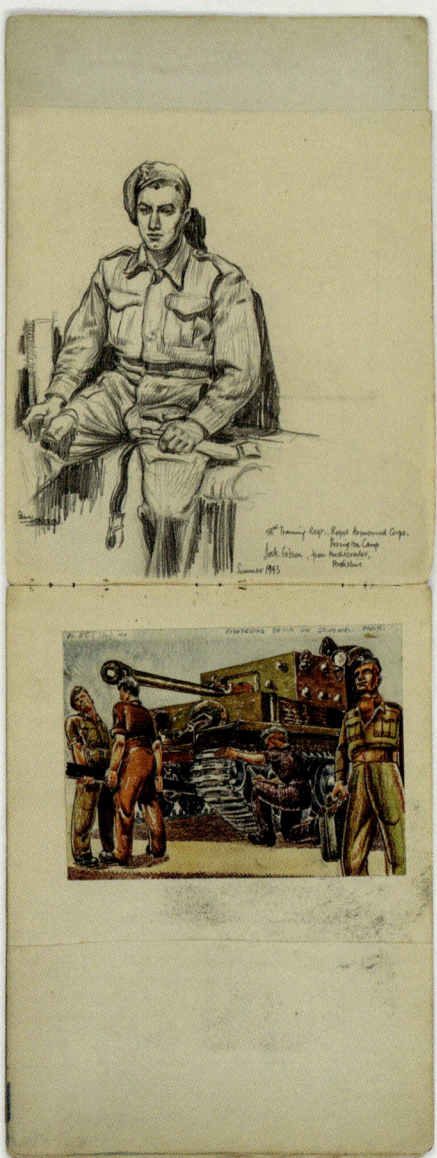

Hewison was born in South Shields, County Durham, on 15 May 1925, the son of a sign maker. He attended South Shields Art School before his military service, training as a gunner and radio operator and joining the 1st Royal Tank Regiment. He wrote a revealing and honest account of his wartime service.

Bill Hewison travelled to Normandy in June 1944, initially tasked with assisting the supply echelon taking fuel up to the tanks in Jerry cans from the various POL (Petrol, Oil and Lubricants) dumps. In July he was ordered forward as a crew replacement. Operation 'Goodwood' was in full swing and Hewison had to replace a corporal in a HQ tank who had to take over another

 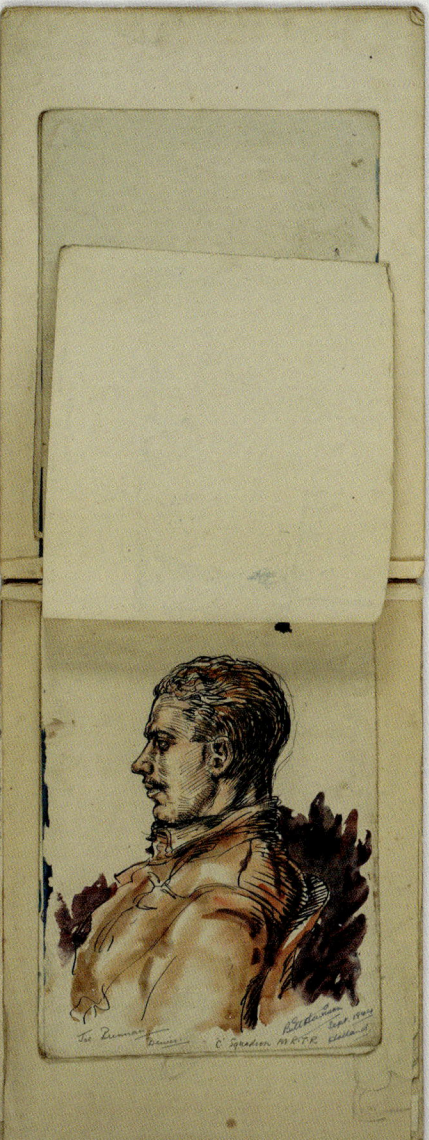 

tank, whose commander had been killed – 'a mordant game of musical chairs' as he recalled. He sketched his fellow tank men and some of the places he visited on his journey across Europe.

The illustration at top right is labelled, 'Ginge Travis w/operator, Ellon, Nr Bayeaux, Normandy, C Squadron, 1 RTR' and dated July 1944. The illustration is 'tipped in' to the sketchbook, meaning it was drawn on a separate piece of paper and added to the sketchbook later. Only one man named Travis served in 1 RTR (the 1st Royal Tank Regiment) so it is assumed this is the portrait of Kenneth Travis (Army number 14221216). Travis survived the fighting but while still serving in Germany with the Army of Occupation in August 1945 he got into difficulty whilst swimming and drowned. He is buried in the Commonwealth War Graves Cemetery in Hamburg.

Bill Hewison ended his own military career in Egypt at GHQ in Cairo. After the war he attended the Regent Street Polytechnic in London to study painting, winning a bronze medal for life drawing. He then trained to be an art teacher, which he carried out part-time allowing him to follow his flair as a cartoonist.

He published his first cartoon in *Punch* in 1950 and went on to become its deputy art editor in 1956, before being appointed as art editor in 1960, selecting cartoons to include and supervising the magazine's layout. He also drew cartoons himself as well as caricatures of theatrical characters.

Bill Hewison – art student to soldier, then an art editor and cartoonist.

#057 E2023.140

CAMOUFLAGE NET

Camouflage for disguise and concealment is as old as warfare itself. Camo net is a simple but effective shape disrupter for armoured vehicles.

From their very first appearance, tanks have been concealed from the enemy by the use of camouflage. Painting vehicles was the first way of trying to blend them into the surrounding landscape, but elaborate schemes were soon covered in mud, which slid down the sides of the tanks. This led to an overall chocolate brown colour being applied.

Soon, netting was being used to disguise vehicles from aircraft and observers. It could hide the distinctive outline of a tank, especially important as tanks needed to be close to the frontline for their deployment. Hessian screens had already been used on the Western Front to hide activity, masking roads or crossing points from being observed.

In the Second World War, nets such as the one illustrated here were made in warehouses and some factories, but many were made by smaller groups of volunteers who were mainly women. Rolls of hessian were delivered with nets from fishing net manufacturers to church and village halls. Hessian strips in different colours were knotted into the twill netting to set patterns; the hessian was treated with a solution to stop any rot when it inevitably got damp in use.

As a group activity, making the nets brought people together with a feeling of involvement in the national war effort. For women, it was also a way of exchanging news of their loved ones away in the services, and keeping up morale. Making nets was also used as a group activity for convalescing servicemen and women.

Modern nets are made of synthetic materials and are intended not just to hide vehicles from the human eye, but also from other detection systems such as thermal imaging.

Making nets — an image used in a book on British women's contribution to the war effort.

#058 E1971.158
CRESTED CHINA TANK

Within days of a photograph of the first tank appearing in the British press, enterprising potteries produced crested china models of Mark I *Crème de Menthe*.

The first image of a tank was published by the *Daily Mirror* on Wednesday 22 November 1916, two months after the first use of tanks in action. This new weapon had been reported in the press but no images were revealed so cartoonists had a field day speculating what the machines would look like.

For having the privilege of printing the first images taken by the official photographer, the *Daily Mirror* paid £500 to an Army charity. The tank photographed was a Mark I named *Crème De Menthe*, which was hit by artillery fire on its approach to the frontline and lost one of its two rear wheels. It was photographed and filmed heading forward to attack a sugar factory where Canadian troops were held up. It helped them capture the position. For his action that day the tank's commander, Captain Arthur Inglis, was awarded the Distinguished Service Order.

The war brought a new demand for souvenirs and from early on there was a general understanding this was a momentous national event that all seemed to want to record and remember. Crested China models were made of battleships, aircraft, soldiers, guns – and of course the new tank.

As mould-makers had only the image of *Crème de Menthe* to copy, the first model tank came out with just one wheel added to the rear. This was later corrected to two wheels. It is thought that because of the popularity of the tank, more examples of tanks in crested china were manufactured than any other subject in the First World War.

The cover of the *Daily Mirror* from 22 November 1916, showing *Crème de Menthe* going into action with one rear wheel. The Tank Museum's model bears the crest of the Lincolnshire village of Freiston.

#059 E1985.90

THE 'FURY' TANK

The Tank Museum's M4A2 Sherman starred in the film *Fury* that went to number 1 at the box office on its release in the USA, followed by top ranking in the UK, Australia, Finland and Ukraine.

Sometimes historic vehicles get another life through their use in films. The Tank Museum was approached in 2013 by Norman Productions, a film company looking for material to be used in a forthcoming war film. The company visited the museum to look at a range of items that might assist them in the production, including imagery of tanks, equipment and actual vehicles to hire.

The script was sent to the curator to read, not so much for guidance to the production company, but so the museum could ascertain what sort of film was being made. As an independent charity, the museum recognised the benefit of being involved in a Hollywood-financed war film. There was potentially money to be made, but more importantly, the chance to make the museum more famous; however, there were also reputational issues to consider.

The film's director, David Ayer, and key crew members visited the museum in the summer of 2013 to look at the museum's M4A2 (76) Sherman to play the role of the 'Hero' tank. This Sherman had been a regular runner in 'Tanks in Action' displays for a long time, often crewed by Second World War veterans Harry Webb and Ron Huggins. The film company also began delicate negotiations to see if Tiger 131 might also be borrowed for some filming. Major discussions were had at the museum, including with the trustees, concerning the risk of involvement. The main issue was around Tiger 131, which had been restored with assistance from the Heritage Lottery Fund and other donors – could the vehicle really be 'safe' on a film set?

Ultimately, an agreement was reached with the production company to lay a concrete pad in the field where the Tiger would be used (hidden by a layer of soil), and the number of gear changes, engine starts, etc were clearly specified in a contract. The Sherman would be away from the museum for six months, crewed by museum staff members Buzz Aldridge and Brian Frost, who would become integrated with the crew and actors.

A deal was struck with the film makers that included provision for the museum to create an exhibition on its involvement using original props. The 'Fury' tank was kept in its 'costume' and is still a popular exhibit, having been seen by millions in the film. In 'making the museum more famous', the Sherman tank in *Fury* certainly accomplished its job.

#060 E1989.92

TANK IN TOWN POSTER

Towns and cities the length of Britain vied with one another to raise money for the war effort. Eye-catching posters were designed to publicise Tank Week events.

Public fascination with the tank in Britain was encouraged further when, for the first time, tanks were driven through London streets at the Lord Mayor's parade in November 1917. The publicity led to the National War Savings Committee realising that there was a great opportunity to use the tank to help raise more money for the war effort, and in turn it created wider support for the armed forces at a crucial time in the conflict. The winter of 1917–18 was bitterly cold, food supplies became limited and with Russia leaving the war, there was an expectation of a major new German offensive in 1918.

A tank was set up in Trafalgar Square on 26 November and a number of celebrities were invited to purchase War Bonds from the door of the tank and give encouraging speeches from the top of the vehicle. The Trafalgar Square Tank Bank raised £3m in two weeks. This success led to three tanks being sent across the country, with towns and cities being encouraged to outdo each other in raising money. Manchester raised nearly £4m, Bradford over £4m, Bristol £1m.

Scouts would put up posters, such as the example opposite, in advance of the event. The tanks were taken by rail to the town station, off-loaded and driven to a prominent position such as the main square or outside the town hall, often accompanied by bands and parades. Speeches were made by a cross-section of the political spectrum, church leaders and local figures, songs were sung and a carnival atmosphere encouraged. Interest in the tank was widespread; Virginia Woolf recorded in her diary on 4 April 1918: 'Richmond worshipping a Tank was like the hum of bees round some first blossom'.

Posters such as this example were produced with a blank area in which to print details of the local event, with stocks carried around the country in advance of the visit. The War Bonds campaign raised £1 billion between October 1917 and September 1918, helped greatly by the appearance of the tank.

Fundraising using tanks took place around the country. Here is a lapel flag from Bristol's Tank Week in December 1917. It featured the Mark IV tank, No 119, *Old Bill*, previously displayed in Cardiff, which was transported to Bristol by rail and positioned opposite the Cathedral on College Green.

At dawn on 20 November 1917, Lieutenant General Hugh Elles led almost 400 tanks into action at Cambrai. Determined to prove the value of the tank to the military hierarchy, he led from the front in a tank named *Hilda*, flying the new regimental colours. This is the actual flag that Elles flew from his tank, which is on display at The Tank Museum. The colours of brown, red and green remain those of the Royal Tank Regiment today.

#061 E1968.81.1
CAMBRAI FLAG

'From mud, through blood, to the green fields beyond' was Lieutenant Colonel J.F.C. Fuller's interpretation of the colours on the battle flag of the new Tank Corps in 1917.

The need to unify the men who served in the new unit that crewed the tanks was apparent to its commander, Lieutenant Colonel Hugh Elles. He was appointed to the role in September 1916, shortly after the first tank attack. Elles asked for a badge to identify those serving with the tanks and in March 1917 a new cloth badge was approved – the outline of a Mark I tank without rear wheels, to be worn on the right jacket sleeve.

In July 1917, the new unit was given the title the Tank Corps and a new cap badge was designed, also sporting an image of the tank. The suggestion of 'Dread Naught' for a motto was changed to 'Fear Naught' by J.F.C. Fuller, the 'brains' of the new force and Elles's Chief-of-Staff.

Elles visited the town of Cassel in northern France with one of his brigade commanders, Lieutenant Colonel John Hardress-Lloyd. In a draper's shop they took what material was available to them – brown, red and green silk. These colours were placed together horizontally to create a flag and Fuller came up with the interpretation of the colours as 'From mud, through blood, to the green fields beyond'.

At the Battle of Cambrai on 20 November 1917, as the tanks from H Battalion readied to move across the start line, 'a lithe figure strode past the infantry and the rear rank tanks, pipe aglow, and an ash stick with mysterious cloth wrapping tucked under his arm...', the commander of H Battalion, Major Gerald Huntbach, recalled. Elles said, 'This is the centre of our line, and I'm going over in this tank'. The tank was called *Hilda* and Elles went forward into action, head out of the roof hatch, the flag of the Corps flying with him. *Hilda* ditched in a trench before the village of Ribecourt and Elles was later seen returning to his headquarters at Beaucamp, flag and pipe still in hand and 'behind him, at a respectful interval, came several crowds of German prisoners'.

Hugh Elles serving as an officer in the Royal Engineers on the Western Front before his transfer to the tanks.

#062 E1983.314

THE GRAINCOURT GUN

The Graincourt gun was captured during a remarkable action fought in front of Graincourt village by the Tank Corps during the Battle of Cambrai in November 1917.

As the British attack began on 20 November 1917, two German field guns had been brought up and placed in front of the village of Graincourt. The guns opened fire as the British tanks advanced, taking out several of their number. Without support from the infantry who were pinned down by machine-gun fire from inside the village, two tanks of the 7th Battalion, *Gorgonzola II* and *Gordon II*, worked around the village and destroyed the machine-gun positions. With the German field guns still firing onto the advancing tanks, *Gordon II* scored a direct hit on the left gun. Lieutenant Baker, commander of *Gorgonzola II*, pressed on towards the right-hand gun position, drove off the gun crew and captured the gun (see *top picture opposite*).

128 THE TANK MUSEUM IN 100 OBJECTS

One of the first German reactions to the British tank attacks in 1916 was the formation of 50 new batteries of 'close combat' artillery. These units were equipped with 7.7cm Feldkanone 96 n.A. guns fitted with one-metre diameter wheels instead of the usual 1.36m wheels as shown on this example. This smaller wheel was so the guns could be easily hidden in emplacements near the frontline. The intention was that they would only be revealed for use should a tank attack occur. A lack of significant attacks following the first one in September 1916 led to the disbandment of these new batteries in May 1917.

At the Battle of Cambrai in November 1917, British attacks near the village of Graincourt were stalling. The infantry commander in the sector was 26-year-old Roland Boys Bradford – amazingly, already a brigadier-general and a Victoria Cross recipient. Six tanks had been knocked out near the village, but on 20 November Bradford organised a new attack with the three tanks that remained.

One of the three vehicles involved was G29, Gorgonzola II, of 7th Battalion, Tank Corps, commanded by Lieutenant Albert Baker MC. Choosing a new route to approach the defending German field guns, Baker succeeded in capturing the guns – adding a bar to his MC in the process. One of the guns was recovered, which is the gun seen here. In 1938, it was presented to the Tank Corps as a trophy from the battle and became known as 'the Graincourt gun'. It was given to The Tank Museum in 1951.

At some point before the flag was acquired by The Tank Museum, the circular central section bearing the swastika symbol and the signatures of soldiers from the 11th Armoured Division was detached from its red background.

130 THE TANK MUSEUM IN 100 OBJECTS

#063 E1995.6
CAPTURED SWASTIKA FLAG

Swastika flags were keenly sought after as war trophies by Allied soldiers as they advanced on Germany.

Flags as symbols of nations or fighting forces have always been a target to capture and popular souvenirs for soldiers to take back home.

This swastika flag has written on it 'CAPTURED AT LUNEBURG (DEUTSCHLAND) BY THE FEW 21/4/45' and a number of 'The Few' have signed their names on the flag:

'Dave Hobbs from the Smoke, Charlie from East Ham, Cpl Barrett, Brighton Sussex, Billie Coyne, Middlesbrough, Geordie, Newcastle, Jack Harrison 'I didn't know it was a Quarter to six', 'AGAIN THE 11th ARMOURED DIVISION DOES IT. WOT A MOB!! GOSH! OH ME!'

The 11th Armoured Division, under the command of 37-year-old Major General 'Pip' Roberts, had fought in Normandy, swept into Belgium and Holland as part of the Great Swan, saw action as flank guards in the Market Garden operation, took part in the clearing of the Rhine approaches and after crossing the Rhine battled towards the River Elbe, reaching Lüneburg on 18 April, a few days before the flag was signed by the various soldiers. More fighting would occur before the Germans surrendered to Montgomery at Lüneburg Heath on 4 May, but the soldiers knew victory was in sight and their thoughts could turn away from fighting – evidenced by Pete Stewart's comment on the flag, 'Get up them stairs wifie'.

This souvenir of a moment in time that brought these 'few' together ended up at a car boot sale in the 1990s. The purchaser kindly donated the flag to The Tank Museum as a suitable permanent home in 1995.

Flags were always a popular souvenir – and tank crews at least had some space on their vehicles to carry off such items.

Walter Carruthers' Webley Mark VI .455 revolver showing the shrapnel damage sustained by its barrel from an exploding shell. The grip that was also damaged is missing.

#064 E1990.49
WEBLEY MARK VI REVOLVER

Private Walter Carruthers' life may have been saved by his Webley Mark VI when the revolver took shrapnel from an exploding shell.

Webley revolvers were in British service from 1887 to 1963; this Mark VI version was used from 1915 to 1923. The bullet size of .455 was large but plenty of skill and practice was needed to fire the gun accurately over any sort of distance – 34yds (30m) was considered a very good range. Officers bought their own guns and enlisted men were issued with the gun. The Webley was rugged and performed well in the mud and wet of the Western Front.

In order to reload the weapon, a catch was released to break open the gun, allowing the six empty brass cases to be automatically extracted. A device called the Prideaux speed loader could be used for getting six bullets straight into the gun, rather than the time-consuming process of placing one bullet at a time. Tank crews carried the gun in a leather holster, sometimes with a lanyard fixed to the butt and circled around the neck or shoulder in case the weapon was dropped. This proved unpopular inside tanks with so many protrusions for a lanyard to catch on.

This Webley revolver belonged to Walter Carruthers of the Tank Corps. After the war he joined Cheshire Constabulary.

This particular gun was used by Private Walter Carruthers, later a member of B Company, the Tank Corps Field Battalion. Carruthers was wearing the revolver when on a reconnaissance mission with an officer. He recalled 'a shell exploded fairly close. I fell and when I got up I found that a piece of shrapnel had shattered the barrel and the handle grip of the revolver.' Carruthers survived the war and went on to serve 30 years as a constable (PC 442) in the Cheshire Constabulary, retiring in January 1951. His family donated the damaged gun to the museum in 1990.

#065 T2006.742

DILLON'S WALKING STICK

There are occasions when an artefact can bridge the years and help provide that connection with a past event – like the Battle of Cambrai.

Colonel Norman Margrave Dillon MC (1896-1997). He became the last surviving Tank Corps veteran of Cambrai.

In the old wooden huts that were used as The Tank Museum artefact stores for many years, I remember coming across this stick in a tea chest. It was surrounded by swagger sticks and Ash plants – the symbol of a Tank Corps officer that dates back to the first attacks when sticks were carried to test the firmness of the ground for tanks to travel over. Reading the spidery handwritten label on this particular piece gave me a frisson of excitement and connection with history.

'This Walking Stick Was Shot From My Hand Whilst Following The Tanks Of B Company 2nd Battalion At Cambrai On 20th November 1917. I Was Company Reconnaissance Officer. The Bullet Split My Thumb And Knocked This Stick 20 Yards Away. I Went On To The Objective And Returned To The Dressing Station.
N M Dillon.'

Norman Margrave Dillon – often called Mark – lived until 1997, when he died aged 101. In later life he was interviewed about the Cambrai attack of November 1917. 'Out of the blue came a bullet and split my thumb in two, it knocked my walking stick miles out of my hand and I thought this is very annoying. I don't know where it came from or who fired it, I never have made it out.'

Damage from the bullet's impact can be seen on the crook of the stick.

Colonel Norman Margrave Dillon's walking stick that he took with him at Cambrai was blown from his hand by a German bullet, which split his thumb in two.

#066 E2006.883.3
THE RPG-7

In over 60 years of service, more than nine million examples of the Soviet-designed RPG-7 portable, reusable anti-tank rocket-propelled grenade launcher have been made and sold worldwide.

The RPG-7 – which in Russian means Ruchnoy Protivotankovvy Granatomyot or hand-held anti-tank grenade launcher – is a further development of the 1949 RPG-2, which itself is derived from the German Panzerfaust and US Bazooka. The muzzle-loaded smoothbore tube is 950mm long and has a diameter of 40mm.

RPG-7 launchers have been used around the world in countless conflicts since their first use in the Middle East in 1967. Estimates put production at over nine million, which is a truly prolific number.

The RPG-7 provides a cheap and simple anti-armour capability, firing a hollow charge warhead that can penetrate up to 500mm of armour. It has also benefitted from a series of newly developed projectiles, including a tandem warhead example for use against reactive armour.

Designed in the Soviet Union, the RPG-7 was a replacement for the earlier RPG-2, itself a Soviet response to the wartime German Panzerfaust. The intention of the designers was to combine the best of the Panzerfaust and the American Bazooka. Soviet forces first received the RPG-7 in 1961 and it was sold and given to many communist allies, with production extended to nine other countries.

To use the launcher, the hollow charge warhead is screwed to a propellant charge in a cardboard tube that also houses closed stabilising fins, then loaded into the launch tube. Aimed at the target, once pulled, the trigger ignites an initial black powder charge that forces the projectile forward at 117m/sec. This movement in turn ignites the sustainer motor, which increases the speed of the warhead to 294m/sec, with the stabilising fins deployed. If the warhead does not hit a target by 900m or in about 4 seconds flying time, it will self-destruct. Accuracy after 200m is poor. Firing the weapon creates a distinctive smoke and dust cloud and a smoke trail behind the rocket, so a swift repositioning of the firer is recommended.

This example is called the 'al Nasirah', an Iraqi-made copy of the RPG-7. Some of those captured in the 2003 Second Gulf War were brought to Britain for analysis by the testing facility at Fort Halstead in Kent. At the end of this process The Tank Museum acquired several.

#067 T2006.2154

17-POUNDER DISCARDING SABOT AMMUNITION

Mounting the 17pdr gun in the Sherman Firefly firing APDS shells was an inspired decision and gave crews a hard-hitting anti-tank weapon.

A tank's purpose is to carry a weapon across the battlefield and deliver the weapon's projectile accurately on target. Different kinds of ammunition are needed for different types of target. The development of new ammunition types (or 'natures') can help increase the lethality of a weapon. For tanks, the race to have projectiles that could penetrate thicker armour became a key development feature in the Second World War.

The inside of a Tiger I turret, penetrated by a 17pdr Discarding Sabot round. This is the rear of the turret where the armour is 82mm thick.

Design of the 17pdr gun was begun in April 1941, but no tank was then capable of carrying it, so it first saw action in February 1943 as a towed anti-tank gun. Developments of ammunition types for the gun led from the basic Armour Piercing round (AP) to an Armour Piercing Capped projectile (APC). This had a soft-nose cap added over the harder metal projectile to stop it shattering on initial impact. Because the cap needed to be blunt in shape it led to the development of a covering ballistic cap to give it better aerodynamics. This was the Armour Piercing Capped Ballistic Cap projectile (APCBC).

A further development was the idea of the 'sabot' round or Armour Piercing Discarding Sabot (APDS). In the 1930s, the French Edgar Brandt Company had started to make rounds with a heavier core and a lighter surrounding 'sabot' or shoe. Brandt engineer Monsieur L. Permutter escaped to Britain in 1940 where, with Mr S.W. Coppock, he worked on improving the design at the Armaments Research Department, Fort Halstead. Here, a lighter casing of Bakelite or an alloy was made to be discarded as soon as the projectile left the barrel, leaving the dense core of tungsten to fly towards the target with the full force of the propellant. The shot had less range and less accuracy beyond 500yds, but far greater penetration. APDS ammunition was issued for the 6pdr gun before D-Day and as ammunition for the 17pdr in August 1944. The 17pdr APDS projectile travelled at 1,200m/sec (the next fastest 17pdr projectile, the APCBC, was 400m/sec slower), and it could penetrate a third more armour at 500m. About 6 per cent of 17pdr ammunition issued was APDS, providing an armour-piercing capability that could defeat any German tank.

A 17pdr Armour Piercing Discarding Sabot (APDS) round. The colour code rings of white/red/blue/white on the tip of the round reveal it to be an APDS T Mk 1B/T, the 'T' standing for tracer. This is also denoted on the shot by the red stencilled 'T' with sloping shoulders above.

#068 E2007.216

MODEL OF HM LCT 7051

More than 800 Landing Craft, Tank (LCT) were used on D-Day, making them the most numerous of all Allied vessels used in the landings.

At 192ft in length, the full-size LCT Mk 3 was the longest in its class. It could carry 11 Valentines, or 11 M4 Sherman medium tanks or 5 Churchill infantry tanks.

Temporary Sub Lieutenant Tony Robinson, RNVR, commander of LCT 7051 and the maker of this detailed 59cm-long scale model.

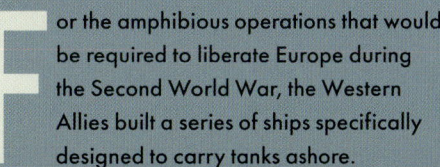

For the amphibious operations that would be required to liberate Europe during the Second World War, the Western Allies built a series of ships specifically designed to carry tanks ashore.

LCT 7051 was a Landing Craft Tank (LCT) Mark 3 that was built by Smith's Dock Co Ltd at South Bank-on-Teeside, and launched on 13 March 1944. The LCT had a shallow draft to allow it to approach a beach and deploy the front ramp to offload vehicles directly onto the foreshore. It could carry 300 tons of cargo and not just tanks were ferried ashore by LCT 7051, but soft-skin vehicles like lorries and jeeps, too.

The 11-man crew of LCT 7051 was commanded by a Royal Naval Volunteer Reserve officer, Temporary Sub Lieutenant Tony Robinson. Robinson kept an album of his wartime experiences, charting his training, his commissioning, the orders given to LCT 7051 for D-Day, his routes across the Channel and even the loading dockets for the vehicles he collected and landed in June 1944. There is a message from his mother on the page for D-Day: 'Just a line darling to say we are all thinking about you all the time and wish you all the good luck in the world.... We are so proud ... the whole of England thinking the same.'

Robinson later made this model of LCT 7051 from scrap wood as well as the case in which to house it. The model and the album were presented to The Tank Museum by Tony Robinson's son Kevin in 2007.

Measuring almost 2 feet in length and standing a foot tall, the push-along Action Man Scorpion tank featured moving wheels and tracks, rotating turret with elevating gun, and opening hatches. It came with a choice of decals — one for the Blues & Royals, one for the Life Guards, but in reality, most children stuck them all on as they fancied.

#069 E2019.2272
ACTION MAN SCORPION TANK

Owned or coveted by a certain generation of boys, the Action Man Scorpion tank was one of the most sought-after toys of the 1970s.

The 'Action Man Scorpion Tank has real hatch openings for two Action Man soldiers. Moving tracks and revolving turret add real excitement to the armoured division.' So said the advertising literature from Palitoy for catalogue number 34710. The plastic toy was a fairly accurate depiction of the British Army's Scorpion light tank in 1/6th scale, and was made from 1972 to around 1983. In 1974, there followed an Action Man Tank Commander with a Royal Tank Regiment black beret.

Action Man was first produced by Palitoy of Coalville in Leicestershire in 1966. The figure was a licenced copy of the successful American 'GI Joe' toy that had come out two years earlier, made by the Hasbro Toy Company. Action Man was an instant success and became the 'Boys' Toy of the Year' in 1966, when it would have set you back 32 shillings (or £1 12s) to buy one.

Around 40 vehicles – helicopters, boats and other craft such as a sledge were made for Action Man, but the Scorpion tank seems to be the item that most remember either owning or coveting. Latterly, at £4.30 it was a costly toy – the most expensive in the Action Man range.

#070 E2018.2340
STANDARD BEAVERETTE

In 1940, several motor manufacturers were asked to produce armoured versions of their basic commercial models. The Standard Motor Company responded with the Beaverette.

The two-man Beaverette was a lightly protected version of Standard's regular 14hp saloon car. Despite its modest armour, it can hardly disguise its civilian origins. This example, a Beaverette Mark IV, was purchased by The Tank Museum in 2018.

After the evacuation of France in June 1940, Britain left behind 331 Light tanks (45 per cent of the Army's holdings), 77 Matilda I and 23 Matilda II tanks (42 per cent of infantry tank holdings) and 184 Cruiser tanks (57 per cent of holdings), in total around half of its total tank strength.

Luckily for Britain the push to increase munitions production had already led to double the output compared to production figures for the first six months of the war. However, the general perception was that 'the cupboard was bare' and desperate measures were needed as although the Army's personnel had in the main been rescued, they lacked equipment to face an imminent German invasion.

Lord Beaverbrook, who was placed in charge of aircraft production in May 1940, instigated the development of an armoured car to defend aircraft factories. The Standard Motor Company was approached and they riveted a simple armoured structure of 11mm plates backed by 3in oak planks onto one of their production cars. The vehicle was open-topped and had no protection at the rear. The next version, the Mark II, managed all-round armour protection, while the Mark III had a shortened chassis and dispensed with the curved front wings from the car. It had top armour and a turret. The Mark IV (seen here) improved on the driver's visibility of the Mark III, but an observer was still needed to help direct the steering. They were fitted with a range of weapons – Bren guns, Boys anti-tank rifles or Vickers 'K' guns.

The Army, RAF and Home Guard used the Beaverette (as it was called), of which some 2,800 were made, but none served abroad. The Beaverette was one of a number of so-called 'emergency measure' vehicles created to meet the threat of German invasion.

A Beaverette patrolling on Queens Road in the centre of Hastings is politely ignored by locals.

#071 E2002.992
NEEDLEWORK BADGE

'Fancy work' was the term coined by British and Empire soldiers in the First World War when they practised needlework as a form of therapy for physical injury or shell-shock.

To help wounded soldiers recover from their injuries, needlework tasks were prescribed at hospitals and convalescent homes. Needlework would allow soldiers to regain dexterity and hand-eye coordination, or to learn to use a left hand instead of right, or vice versa, if a hand was damaged or lost.

Needlework also provided a calming therapy and an end product that could be given to loved ones or saved by soldiers' families. Patterns for embroidery, cushion covers and antimacassars to make at home were printed in a number of magazines during the First World War. Some had simple mottos to copy or cap badges and unit insignia – as can be seen here.

This piece of embroidery, the badge of the Tank Corps, was carried out by Cyril William Christie as part of his convalescence. Christie was a crewman aboard a tank called *Moody Maude*. What his wounds were we are not sure, but the item was kept proudly framed by his daughter before it was donated to The Tank

A portrait of William Christie before his injury.

Museum in 2002. It is thought that Christie had joined the Army underage – he certainly looks very young in his wartime photograph.

#072 A2019.35

DIARIES AND LETTERS

Jake Wardrop was in action with the 5th Royal Tank Regiment from beginning to end of the Second World War, but he was killed in its dying days.

Jake Wardrop (or to give him his full name John Richard Wardrop) joined the Army in 1937 aged 19, having found it hard to settle to a routine job. He trained at Bovington and served on Vickers Mediums with the 5th Battalion Royal Tank Corps at Perham Down, becoming an accomplished boxer in the sport-mad unit.

When war came, the 5th fought in France in 1940 before having to return to Britain via Brest. The reformed unit was then sent to North Africa, and on the journey Jake started a diary that has become a classic memoir of the war. Jake was not happy with formal discipline, regularly getting into scrapes and being demoted in rank on more than one occasion – but on the battlefield he came into his own and saw much action in the desert. One of his tank commanders, Paddy Doyle DSO, MC, who rose to the rank of lieutenant colonel, recalled he 'was a very brave and intelligent person... During one period of some thirty days in 1941 we were shot out of ten tanks with the loss of one or more crew members per tank.... I sincerely believe I owe my survival to Wardrop's prowess and initiative.'

Jake sent his diary home in sections along with letters to his family. In 2019, the family kindly donated these to The Tank Museum.
A transcript of a letter sent to Jake's mother in November 1943 from Italy is also in the collection. It explains his attitude to the war and what to think should he not return. Jake was killed on 10 April 1945, only a few weeks before the war's end.

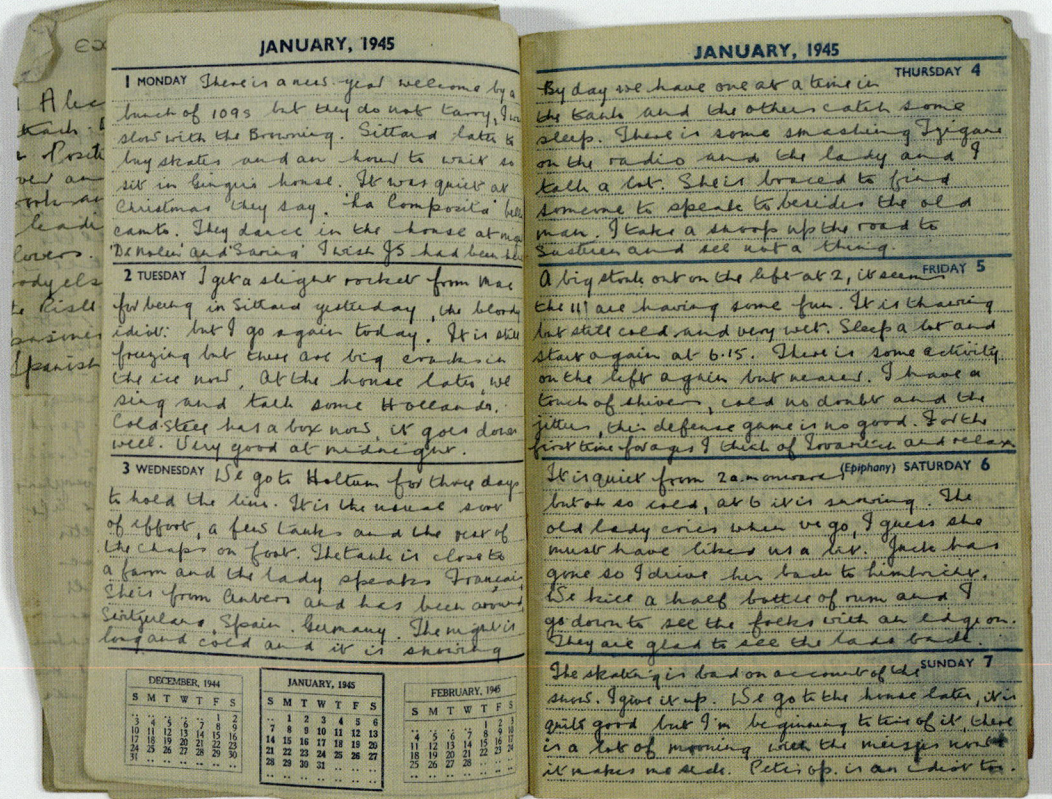

Jake Wardrop wrote letters home and kept a personal diary in a collection of journals and notebooks, using whatever writing materials came to hand, including notebooks of fellow soldiers. They were edited and published posthumously.

A young, cheeky-looking Jake Wardrop, guitar in hand, poses with Royal Tank Corps troopers before the Second World War.

THE TANK MUSEUM IN 100 OBJECTS 149

The Sturmtiger from which the mortar was removed. It is seen here at Chertsey for evaluation along with a Bergepanther. Both vehicles were subsequently scrapped.

After the battle of Stalingrad, Hitler looked for weapons to be used in similar urban sieges. He wanted a howitzer of large calibre that could be fitted on an armoured chassis. No suitable howitzer seemed available so a weapon designed for coastal defence, the RTG38, was adapted.

A prototype vehicle based on a Tiger I was swiftly built to carry the weapon but priority was given to building the Tiger gun tanks. Hitler suggested using damaged Tigers that had been returned from action – 18 were ultimately built, or rebuilt, and called the Sturmtiger.

The new weapon took an enormous shell containing 122.5kg of Amatol explosive, driven out of the gun by 40kg of propellant in a tubular case. The barrel had a cast outer layer and an inner liner 12mm thick. Between the two layers held together at the breech and muzzle there were 32 holes that allowed the propellant gases to be vented forward and so lessen the recoil of the barrel.

Nine rifling grooves in the barrel spun the shell which, depending on weather conditions, could be fired out to 6.5km. Weather, especially temperature, affected the burn rate of the propellant and therefore the range, so the crews were issued with range tables to calculate the fall of shot.

In August 1944, Sturmtigers were used to decimate areas of Warsaw during the heroic uprising, but elsewhere the nature of the fighting as German forces retreated did not give many opportunities for the weapons to be used. One retreating Sturmtiger got stuck in a ditch and was knocked out by advancing US troops at Duren in Germany in February 1945. The tank was later recovered and brought to Britain for analysis at the Chertsey test site. The vehicle was scrapped but the gun was saved and given to The Tank Museum in 2001 by the Royal Military College of Science, Shrivenham.

#073 E2001.1068

STURMMÖRSERWAGEN 606/4 MIT 38CM RW 61

Unlike a conventional gun, the RW 61 fired a rocket-propelled projectile containing a motor that continued to burn after the round had left the barrel.

A Treibsatz 4581 rocket motor allowed the projectile to be fired from a short-barrelled weapon without a loss in range or accuracy. In fact, the RW 61 fired 1.5m projectiles from a barrel just 2m long.

#074 E1964.101
ROYAL TANK CORPS UNIFORM
(1935)

Designed with utility in mind and to suit wear in the confined interior of a tank, the Black Drill, Working Dress (SP 1935) became the template for the 'universal' battledress adopted by the British Army in 1939.

Troopers of the 4th Battalion Royal Tank Regiment carry out pistol practice in their black two-piece uniforms in a farmyard near Arras on 6 October 1939.

The first tank crews wore the standard service dress in their vehicles along with chocolate brown overalls. Not only would overalls protect the uniform from oils and grease, but they also presented less in the way of pockets or belts to snag on projections inside the vehicle.

In 1935, the Royal Tank Corps was issued black two-piece working suits made of hard-wearing cotton drill material. The jacket had two patch pockets, epaulets and was fly-fronted to hide the buttons. It had a built-in belt arrangement that extended from the left side of the jacket to be attached to a brass buckle on the right of the jacket bottom. The trousers had a large patch pocket sewn onto the upper left leg.

This uniform provided a template for the two-piece 'universal' battledress that was adopted by the British Army in April 1939, the uniform that is so familiar in thousands of images of British troops in the Second World War.

The new woollen battledress was beginning to be issued to troops when war began, but many of the BEF who travelled to France in 1939–40 still had the older service dress that looked very much like their fathers' uniforms of the First World War. A reed green denim version of the new battledress, sometimes called Denim Overalls, was also issued for dirty work. The new uniforms led to the end of the black uniform for tank crews, but some Royal Tank Regiment soldiers continued to wear their black uniforms during the following year before they were ultimately replaced. Black overalls were used again by the Royal Tank Regiments from the early 1950s and they continue to be a distinctive outfit for the one remaining regiment in the 21st century.

#075 E1951.25
PANZERBEFEHLSWAGEN
GERMAN COMMAND TANK

This command tank was one of 190 made and was captured in North Africa by British forces. It has battle damage and has been repainted to represent a tank in the earlier 1940 campaign.

A command tank is captured in the Western Desert. Many of the German vehicles in The Tank Museum's collection come from North Africa, which was the first campaign where captured examples could be returned to Britain for analysis.

Although it was a relatively small part of the German Army at the start of the Second World War, the German Panzer force was to play a decisive role in the early campaigns. The reasons for the German success were studied carefully by opposition forces but even today the propaganda images, constantly repeated, give a false impression of overwhelming German numbers and superior military equipment.

Two key German advantages were the concentration of their tank force (which barely equalled the Western Allies in May 1940 and was far smaller than the Red Army's tank force in the summer of 1941), and the successful use of combined arms – the use of tanks, air power, infantry and artillery together to create the best effect. To achieve both of these the German tank arm needed good communications and the *Panzerbefehlswagen* or command tank, played a major role in the early German success.

In the French Army many tanks relied on hand signals and flags, as did the Soviet tank forces. The radios of this command tank allowed communication with the rest of the German tank force (even if some only had receivers and could not reply) and with higher command formations – allowing the swift transfer of information to and from the fighting vehicles and to the other arms involved.

This rapid information exchange gave the German military the ability to react to a changing situation much faster than their opposition and led to a series of early victories that stunned the world. A new phrase, 'Blitzkrieg' or 'Lightning War', was bandied about in the press.

#076 E1949.343

M3 GRANT TANK

The M3 Grant had been unpopular with the Tank Board and Ministry of Supply in the United Kingdom when it was first offered by the US, but in service it proved to be a great success.

The desperate need for tanks by Britain and France in 1939–40 led to purchasing missions heading to the United States. The US Army had been experimenting with tanks and possible designs in the interwar years but had put few into production. Expertise drawn from the US car industry saw the rapid expansion of tank production in 1940–41 but factories had to be built, machine tools and skills acquired and new vehicles designed.

After initial attempts to have the Char B built in the US for the French, and tanks like the Matilda and Valentine, as well as spare parts built for Britain, the US suggested Britain bought into their own new tank programme instead. The desire was to fit a 75mm gun in a turret but US industry was not yet capable of building this (US tanks so far had been fitted with what was then considered an adequate 37mm gun). A tank to act as an interim model, to be called the M3, was designed using the engine and transmission from an earlier M2 model tank. Help was arriving in the form of technical advice from Britain and casting engineers from Le Creusot in France.

Copying the French Char B and first Churchills, the 75mm gun was fitted in the hull with the earlier 37mm high velocity gun in the turret. The British military insisted on having radios in the turret so an alternative deeper cast turret design was produced. In line with Prime Minister Winston Churchill's insistence that tanks should have names for ease of remembering, the British version would be called the M3 Grant tank and the original US version the M3 Lee.

Britain placed a £240 million order to buy 1,250 M3 tanks, representing all its remaining uncommitted reserves. In May 1942, British forces used the Grant for the first time in North Africa. With its 75mm gun, the tank had heavier firepower than most of the opposing German tanks. However, the Grant was a tall tank and the hull-mounted main gun meant it could not be used from a hull-down position, a tactic where the main hull of the tank would be hidden, presenting less of a target but allowing the turret to be used. British crews also liked the protection of its 2in frontal armour and the ease of maintenance.

The tank saw service in North Africa and the Far East but once the M4 Sherman, the tank with the 75mm main armament in the turret was ready, it was swiftly replaced.

The US Army's version of the M3, the Lee, seen on manoeuvres in the USA.

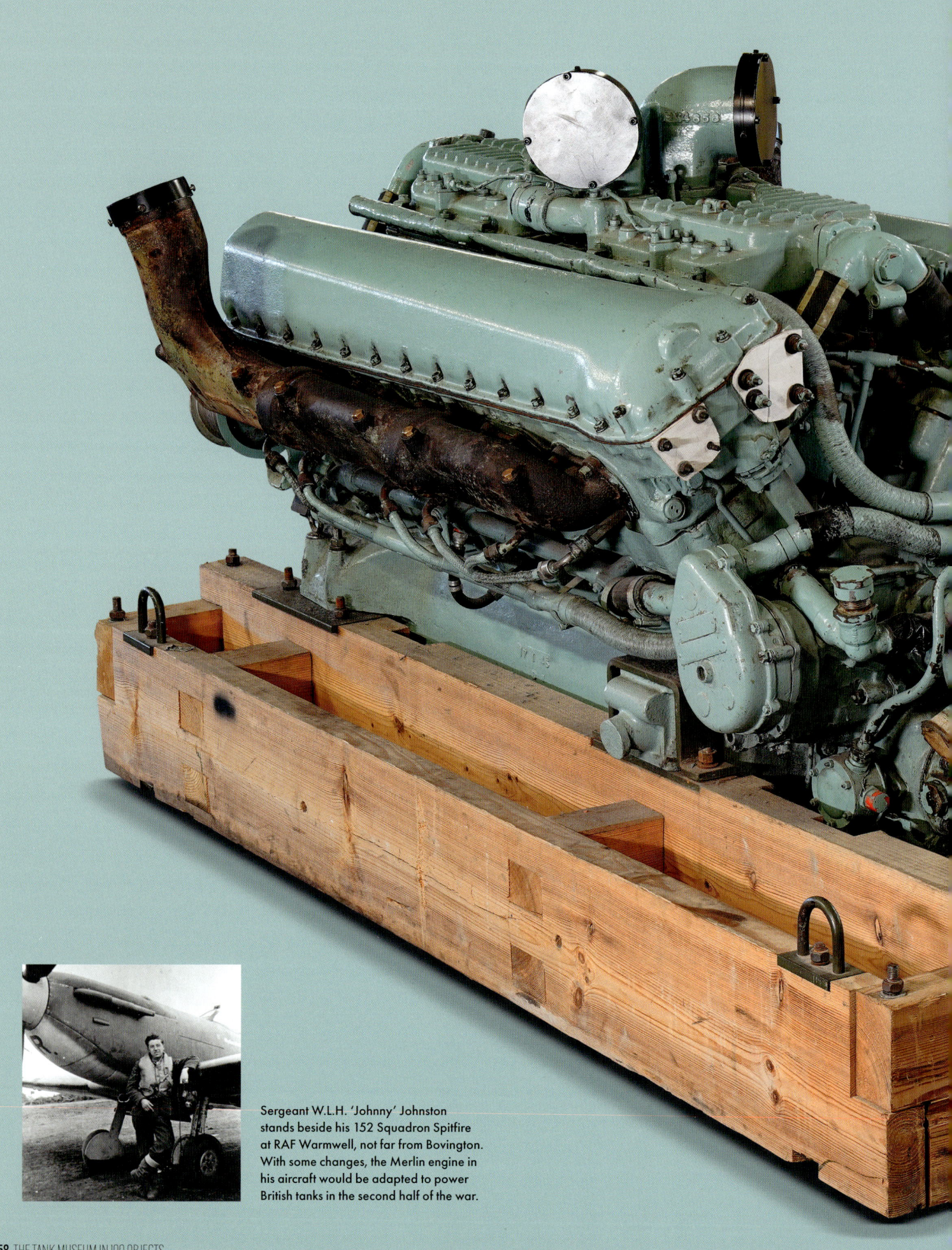

Sergeant W.L.H. 'Johnny' Johnston stands beside his 152 Squadron Spitfire at RAF Warmwell, not far from Bovington. With some changes, the Merlin engine in his aircraft would be adapted to power British tanks in the second half of the war.

#077 E2017.472
ROLLS-ROYCE METEOR ENGINE

Developed from the legendary Merlin that powered the RAF's Spitfire and Lancaster, the Meteor tank engine proved to be just as much a winner as its aero counterpart.

Tax implications of using larger engines had stifled the commercial development of more powerful engines in interwar Britain. The 300hp Liberty engine had been developed in the First World War and was still used in tanks in the early years of the Second, but more power was required as tank weight increased.

The aircraft industry had the Rolls-Royce Merlin engine, which started the war at 1,000hp.

William Rowbotham at Rolls-Royce found the company's Clan Works at Belper and the design team based there were under-utilised and so he started a project with assistance from Leyland engineers to create a suitable tank engine from the successful Merlin aero engine.

Work began with parts salvaged from crashed aircraft, while the direction of the engine rotation had to be changed to match existing gearboxes. Aircraft-specific parts were removed, cast pistons used instead of forged and the engine sump flattened. In April 1941, the new engine made its first test-run in a Crusader tank and an amazing 50mph was achieved. The tank version of the famous Merlin would be called the Meteor.

The withdrawal of Leyland support led Rolls-Royce to approach the Ministry of Supply and the Minister in charge, Lord Beaverbrook, cabled back: 'The British Government has given you an open credit of one million pounds. This is a certificate of character and reputation without precedent or equal. Beaverbrook.'

A new version of the Cromwell tank, the A27M, was designed to house the engine, and this became the main production model. The 550hp Meteor engine gave the tank greater speed and mobility, shown to good effect in the 'Great Swan' breakout from Normandy in 1944. This extra power allowed designers to add a greater weight of armour protection and the engine went on to drive the succeeding Comet and Centurion tanks.

#078 E1980.18

J.F.C. FULLER'S ALBUM

J.F.C. Fuller (1878-1966) was pivotal to the story of armoured warfare. He was also a highly controversial individual who joined the British Union of Fascists and was a great supporter of Sir Oswald Mosley.

J.F.C. Fuller was appointed as a staff officer at the new Heavy Branch, Machine Gun Corps headquarters at Bermicourt in 1916. He already had the nickname 'Boney' — whether because of his high forehead, or Napoleonic brilliance, is not clear. Fuller got on well with Hugh Elles, the Commander of the Tank Corps, and came up with tactics for the use of tanks at the Battle of Cambrai in 1917. This album charts the development of the Tank Corps with reports on the successes and failures of the tanks. It also features copies of orders, reports and the ideas and instructions Fuller gave to develop the new force.

Fuller became an ardent advocate of mechanisation (in the album, one of his articles is entitled 'Petrol vs Muscle' and advocates the use of new technology by military forces). He wrote extensively on the subject and cooperated with theorist Basil Liddell Hart in the interwar period, gaining influential positions as the Chief Instructor at Camberley Staff College in 1923 and then Military Assistant to the Chief of the Imperial General Staff in 1926. Given the opportunity in 1927 of taking command of the Experimental Mechanised Force, some thought he fudged the chance of demonstrating his theories by turning down the role, stating there was not enough staff support. He was still promoted to major general in 1930, but left to write full time in 1933.

The interwar debate of how tanks and mechanised forces were to be used to best effect was played out in military trials, in the press and at conferences. The reactionary view against modernising the Army was often portrayed by the cavalry officer.

J.F.C. Fuller wrote: 'In 1919 I was the sole person who saw war in the form it would be; yet saw it only as an acorn and not as an oak'.

Fuller had an interest in the occult and became a follower of Aleistair Crowley before the First World War. He wrote an essay praising Crowley's poetry and won £100 in a competition. Fuller helped Crowley set up his new occult order A∴A∴ but they later fell out.

In the 1930s, Fuller joined the British Union of Fascists and was a great supporter of Sir Oswald Mosley. He was also invited by Hitler to his 50th birthday parade in April 1939.

A sympathiser of Nazi aims, Fuller was not interned during the Second World War but he was never invited back into military service.

TRENCH CROSSING CAPACITY.
The Tank would undoubtedly have great difficulty
anything wider than two metres.
SITUATION.
SALVAGE.
The Tank would be extremely difficult to salve unless
the line is advanced.
The work would take anything from 2 to 12 hours and
very difficult except in daylight.
SKETCH OF HOSTILE TANK, USED AT VILLERS BRETONNEUX.
on 24th April, 1918
Cab.
Flap
Flap
M.G
M.G.
M.G
Rear
22·9"
Track
Front
Side View
Extreme Width 9'6"
Notes.
Points most vulnerable to Rifle & M.G. Bullets shewn :-
French A.P. bullets have penetrated the Cab. Ordinary Bullets
pass through apertures if flap is open and through
space between Gun shield and front of Tank.
The "splash" of ordinary bullets is effective against Cab,
and against M.G. emplacements.
Armour Plate is of poor quality and there is no protection
against the "splash" of an ordinary bullet.
This Tank cannot cross a large trench (8 feet or over) or
large shell holes.
Artillery. A direct hit will put this Tank out of action.
Headquarters
Tank Corps.
5th May 1918.

Diagram 10.
(Stage 1.)
Sector C.
Sector D.
Sector B.
Advanced Tanks.
Flank Guard Tank.
Main Body Tanks.
Firing Line.
Supports.
Reserves.

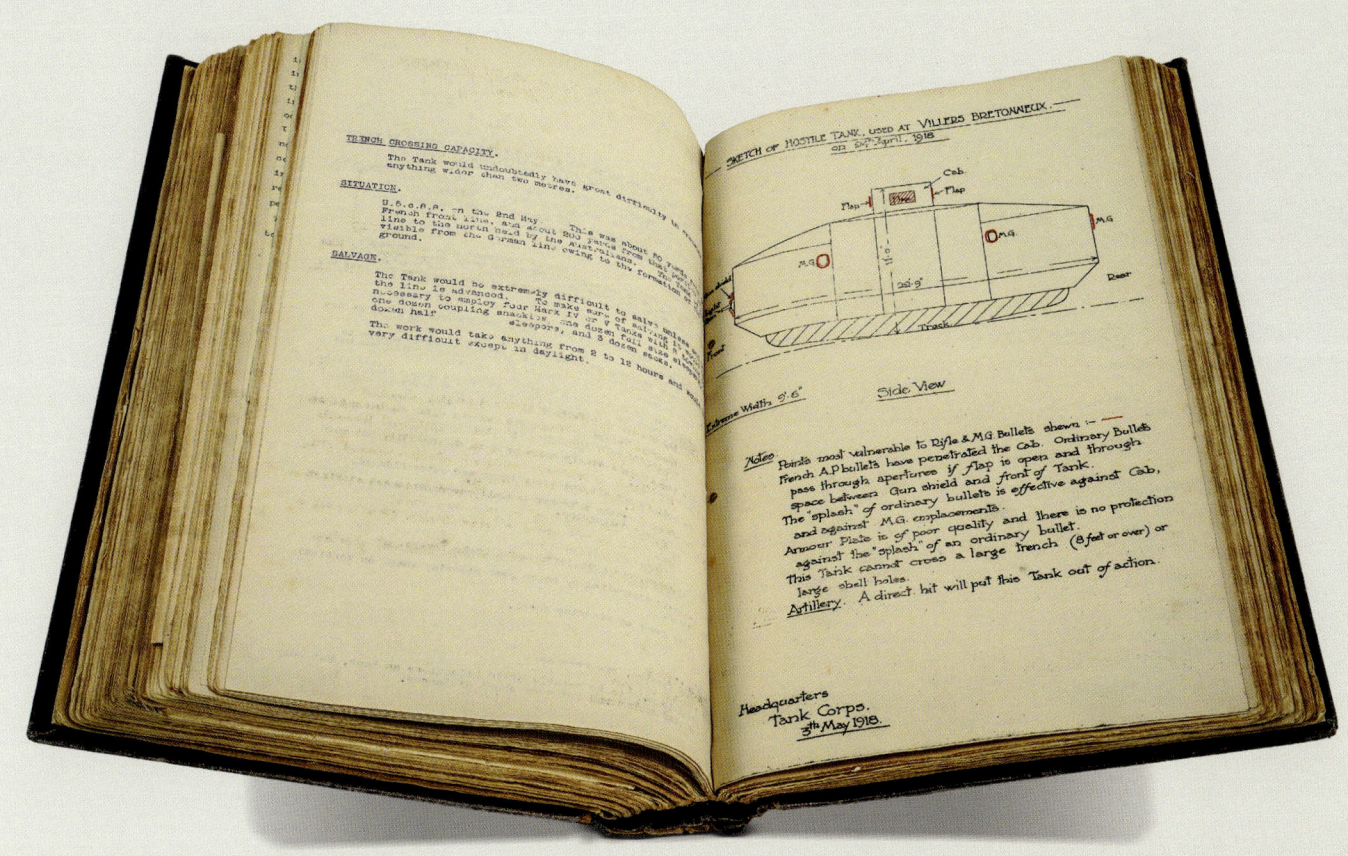

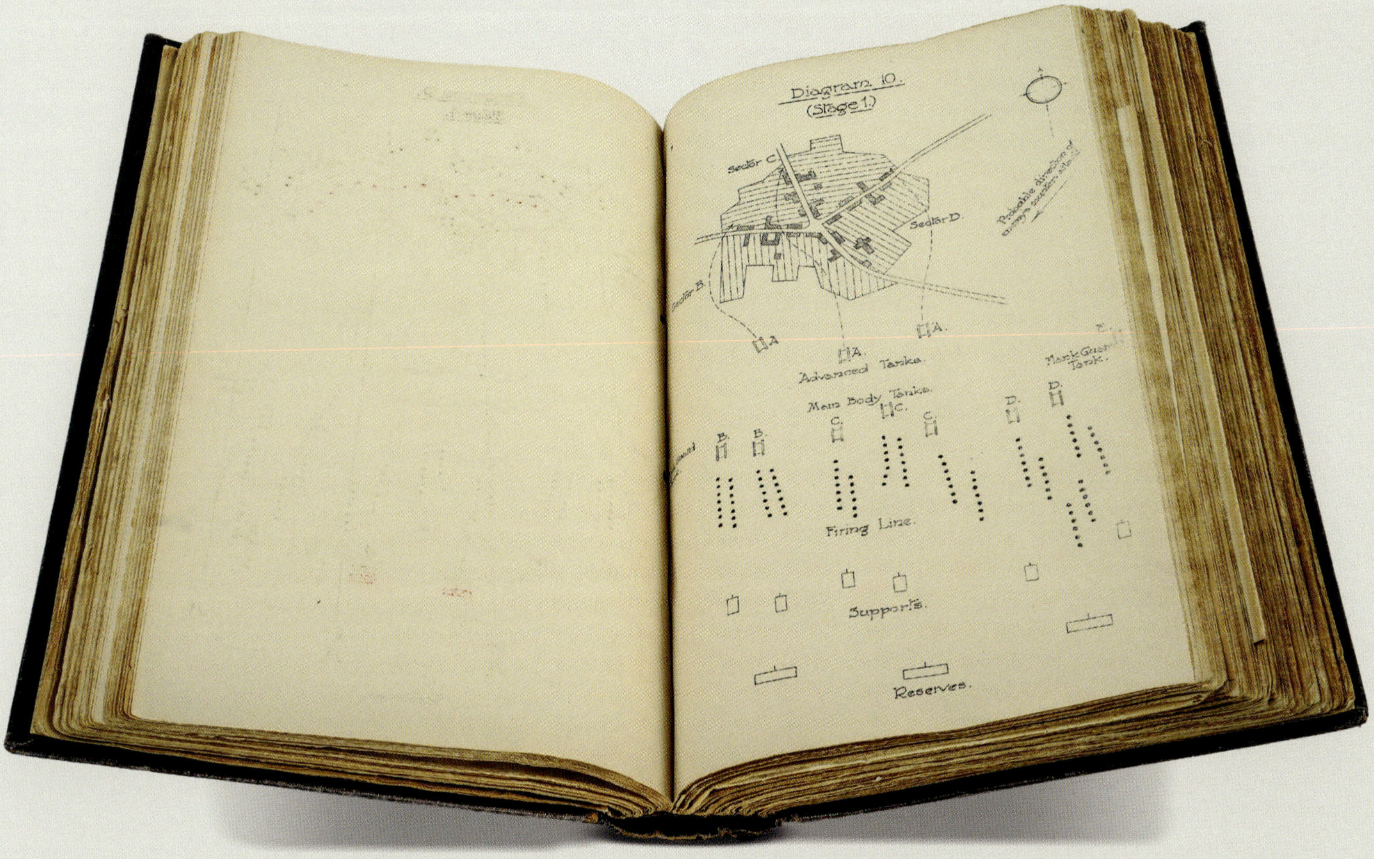

#079 E1952.44

T34/85

The T-34 is arguably the most influential tank ever designed. It has also come to symbolise the determination of the Russian people in 'The Great Patriotic War'.

For understandable reasons some weapons become symbols, sometimes of causes or countries – the 'rebel' brandishing an AK-47 assault rifle or the RAF Spitfire fighter as a symbol of Britain's wartime defiance. For the Russian people the T-34 tank has come to represent the Second World War, known to them as 'The Great Patriotic War', and the sacrifices made.

The T-34 has been praised and lambasted along with the Sherman tank as not an equal to the better-quality German tanks like the Panther. When it first went into production, it was a well-built tank. Designed by Mikhail Koshkin (who died from pneumonia caught whilst testing the prototype), tanks were just reaching the Red Army when Germany invaded the Soviet Union in the summer of 1941. The movement of factory equipment and workers to new sites behind the Ural Mountains away from the advancing German forces led to a realisation that parts of the tank could be dispensed with or simplified. The F-34 76.2mm gun originally had 861 parts – this was reduced to 614 during production and the overall cost of making the T-34 was halved in two years.

Invading German forces were impressed with the T-34 and looked at reproducing it, but built the Panther instead. The T-34 did have many poor features – the original two-man turret meant the commander had to aim and fire the gun in a cramped space; most lacked radios and visibility was poor from inside the vehicle leading to slower engagement times.

A new tank was designed to replace the T-34, the T-43, but rather than stop factories to re-tool the decision was made to build an evolutionary model, the T-34/85, with a new turret allowing for a third crewmember and housing a more powerful 85mm gun.

The sheer numbers produced (over 80,000) made up for the short operational service life and that over 44,000 were destroyed in combat. T-34s went on to serve in Warsaw Pact countries into the Cold War, and some remain in service. In 2020, 30 T-34/85 tanks were donated from Laos to Russia for parades and historical displays – demonstrating how important this tank still is in Russian history.

162 THE TANK MUSEUM IN 100 OBJECTS

#080 E2006.1708.11
ORPEN'S LETTERS TO ELLIOTT HOTBLACK

War Artist Sir William Orpen's visit to the Tanks Corps Headquarters at Bermicourt in 1917 led to an interesting exchange of letters with Intelligence Officer, Elliott Hotblack.

Sir William Orpen (1878–1931) KBE, RA, RHA, was a very successful portrait painter in the pre-First World War period and having powerful contacts in society during that war he was given a commission to paint in France as an Official War Artist. Orpen was inspired by his visits to the frontline and became enamoured with the average British 'Tommy'. As part of his commission he visited the Tank Corps Headquarters at Bermicourt in late 1917 and painted both Major General Sir Hugh Elles, the Tank Corps Commanding Officer, and Major Elliott Hotblack, the Intelligence Officer.

As a major, Elliott Hotblack acted as the Intelligence and Reconnaissance Officer for the Tank Corps. In the Second World War as a major-general he was to lead British forces in Norway in 1940 but suffered a stroke before he could take command.

Orpen described Hotblack in his memoir that was published in 1921, *An Onlooker in France 1917–1919*, as 'mild and gentle, full of charm; one could hardly imagine he had all those DSO's, and wound stripes – Hotblack, who liked to go for a walk and sit down and read poetry. He said it took his mind off devising plans to kill people better than anything else.'

Hotblack wrote to Orpen, and Orpen's replies are in The Tank Museum's Archive. In one of the letters, Orpen wrote that he wanted to get back to the Front but there were 'difficulties'. The difficulties he admitted were because 'I have been naughty'. He had submitted a picture of his beautiful French mistress for exhibition in London, claiming she was a German spy that had been shot by the French military. The British censor challenged the story and after continuing the lie for a period he had to finally admit his falsehood.

In another letter dated 'the 10/10/18', he writes that he has 'Spanish flu and has done little work'. He commiserates with Hotblack who had been wounded again. 'I would have been too scared to paint you in that state,' writes Orpen, and he includes an imagined sketch of a bandaged Hotblack.

Orpen bequeathed all his wartime work to the nation and it now resides in the Imperial War Museum. The generous gift did his longer-term reputation a disservice as only a few works can be exhibited at any one time.

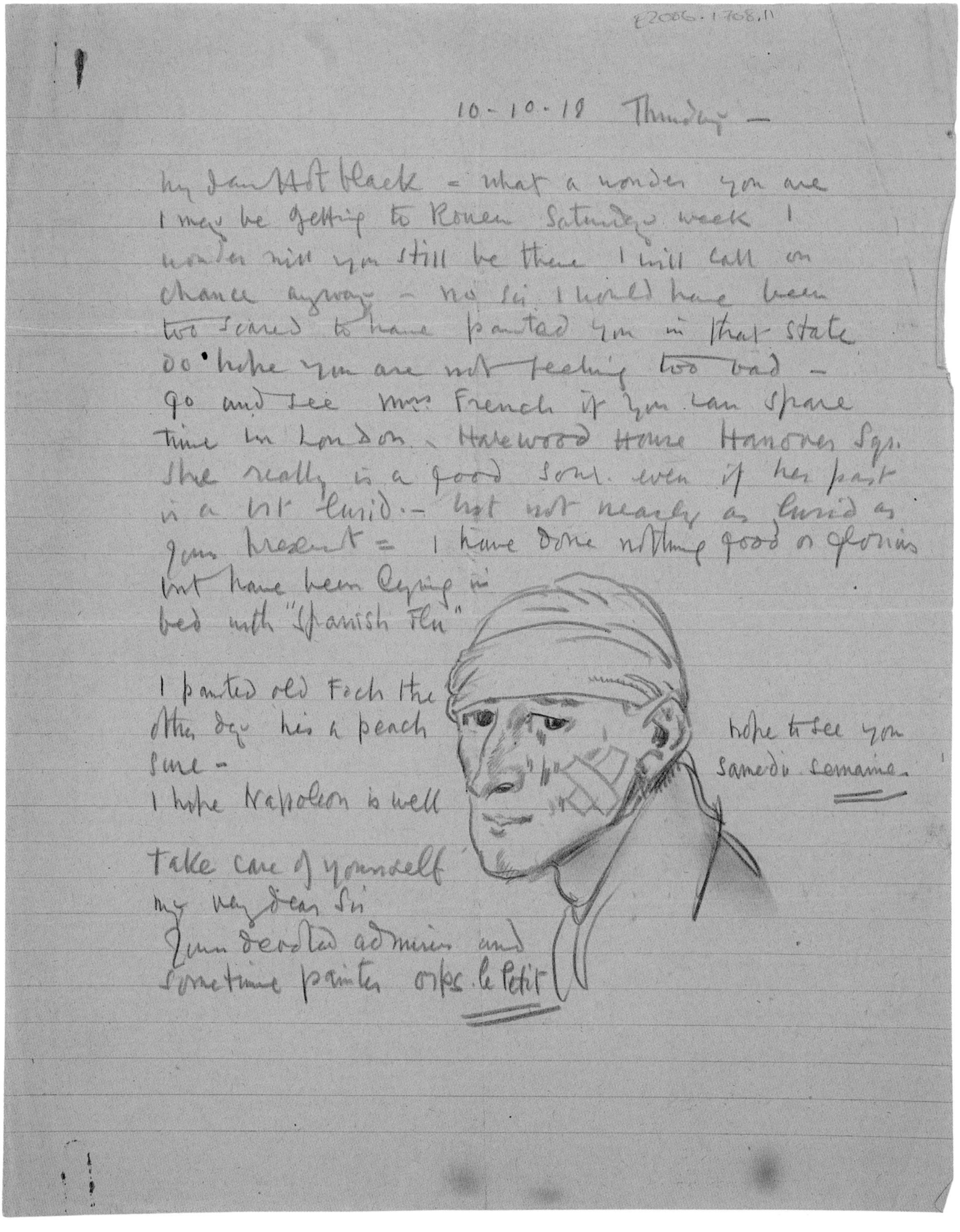

10·10·18 Thursday —

My dear Ht Black — what a wonder you are
I may be getting to Rouen Saturday week I
wonder will you still be there I will call on
chance anyway — No Sir I would have been
too scared to have painted you in that state
Do hope you are not feeling too bad —
Go and see Mrs French if you can spare
time in London, Harewood House Hanover Sqr.
She really is a good soul. even if her past
is a bit lurid. — but not nearly as lurid as
yours present = I have done nothing good or glorious
but have been lying in
bed with "Spanish Flu"

I painted old Foch the
other day his a peach   hope to see you
sure —   samedi semaine.
I hope Napoleon is well

take care of yourself
my very dear Sir
your devoted admirer and
sometime painter Orps. le Petit

#081 E2013.3676

THE BLACK BERET

Following its introduction by the Royal Tank Corps in 1924, the black beret has since become synonymous with the identity of the Royal Tank Regiment.

Dogs appear in countless soldiers' photo albums – this mutt wears an RTR beret, goggles and carries a swagger stick.

The Scottish bonnet or tam o'shanter has sometimes been seen as a forerunner of the military beret in Britain, with clans wearing the headgear against English troops in the 17th and 18th centuries. In the 1880s, the French Mountain Troops or Chasseurs Alpins adopted a large, floppy, dark blue, beret. It was these berets that Hugh Elles, commander of the Tank Corps, saw and tried on in May 1918 when Chasseurs Alpins troops were stationed nearby.

In 1922, Elles recommended the beret for use by the Tank Corps. During the war it had been found that the Field Service Cap, which had a peak, was not practical in a tank as the peak would knock it off the head of the wearer if they put their eye to a sight or vision block. Blue was replaced by black in the final design, a dark colour that would hide the inevitable oil stains likely inside a tank. A large beret, although not as floppy as the French example, was chosen and approved for wear in March 1924. There were initial jokes

about Royal Tank Corps members being taken for French onion sellers, but the beret along with the tank arm badge gave a sense of identity.

A decade later the German Panzertruppen arm also adopted a large black beret – the *Schutzmütze*. This was roomy enough for a protective skull cap to be worn inside it. In 1940, the practical beret was taken up by the rest of the British Army to replace the Field Service Cap in a variety of colours to represent different corps and units – the most famous being maroon worn by airborne forces and green of the Army Commandos.

This black beret belonged to Sergeant Donald Featherstone (1918–2013) who served in North Africa and Italy during the Second World War. He wrote a memoir of his experiences in battles such as Cassino that is held in The Tank Museum's Archive, as well as establishing himself as an author of many books on wargaming and military history.

#082 E2007.426
MECHANISATION POSTCARD

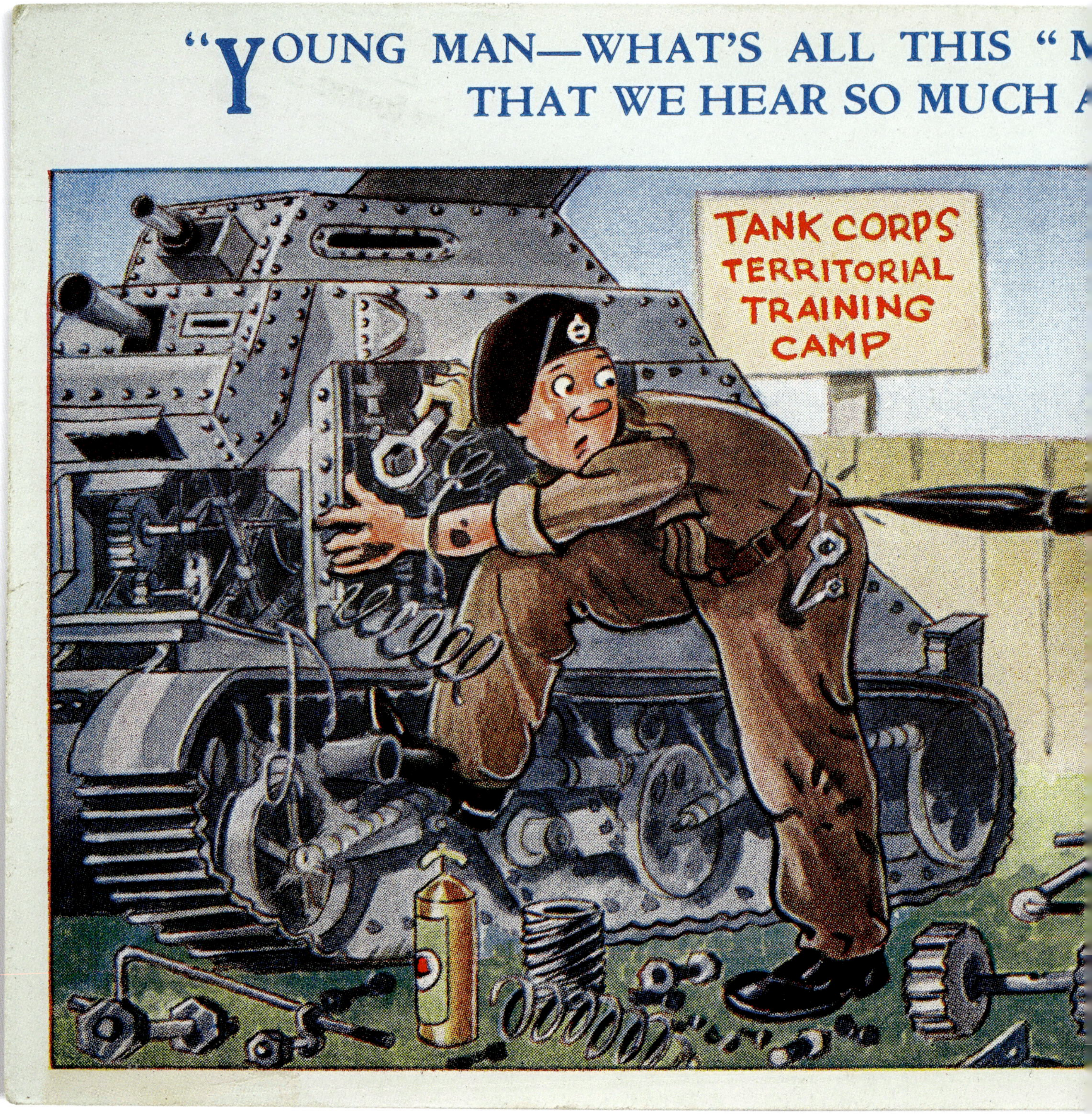

Britain entered the Second World War as the most mechanised Army in Europe, but with a bewildering array of tanks in service and development, and no cohesive sense of direction.

The mechanisation of the British military in the interwar period was a topic that reached the general public in a variety of ways, including as seen here with a popular postcard. Granny asks a Royal Tank Corps trooper to explain 'what's all this mechanisation we hear so much about?'

Between the wars the level of interest in the forces in popular culture was far greater than the current era. Many, of course, had served in the First World War or had family who did, and the services appeared in newsreels and events such as tattoos and Empire Day on a regular basis. The transition of the cavalry from the horse to armoured vehicles was a ready subject for cartoons and jokes with plenty of stereotypes for the humourist to draw on. The new Royal Tank Corps was seen as the forward-looking but more plebeian force as opposed to the romantic and aristocratic cavalry.

'The Royal Tank Regiment ... is a creation apart; it is composed of the rude mechanicals who despise horses,' wrote Robert Sherriffs in his book, *Salute if You Must*.

In his 1936 Parliamentary address, the Secretary of State for War, Alfred Duff Cooper, announced the mechanisation of eight cavalry regiments. 'It is like asking a great musical performer to throw away his violin and to devote himself in future to a gramophone.' But he continued, 'It is a great sacrifice for the cavalry men, but it has been accepted in the very best spirit, practically without protest, by all the regiments concerned'.

Despite the humour and the portrayal of the Army, the High Command and the cavalry in particular as being reactionary and hidebound – the level of mechanisation in the British Army on the eve of the Second World War was a remarkable success.

#083 E1968.114
QAIMNS NURSE'S CAPE

Souvenir collecting has been perennially popular among military personnel since time immemorial. QAIMNS nurse Jenny Lindsaye's cape conceals a wealth of badges (even several German ones).

Collecting souvenirs is a long tradition for those in military service. This nurse's cape belonged to Captain Jenny Lindsaye of the 49th General Field Hospital, which was set up in Normandy six days after D-Day. It was the first to include women – members of Queen Alexandra's Imperial Military Nursing Service (QAIMNS). The cape shows, on the inside, a scarlet lining with a profusion of cloth formation signs and shoulder badges. The tradition was for soldiers to donate a cloth badge to the nurse that looked after them. Some capes, like this one, show badges from enemy troops that had been nursed, too. No one knows when exactly the collecting of badges to decorate a cape started, but a number of such capes appear in the military auction rooms each year and it is likely the practise was quite widespread.

The key role of nurses in wartime was, of course, to help soldiers recover as swiftly as possible from injury or illness and if possible return to service. Of course, their role in helping troops recover was also a matter of morale. Memoirs show how some feminine warmth and attention in the horrors of war gave wounded men a sense of better things, a reason to go on.

This cape also shows a constant problem that museums have to face. The item was displayed in a case for many years and now shows the effect of light on the fabric. It has permanently faded, showing a distinct colour loss in some areas – less so where the fabric was folded. Items are collected for public benefit and of course there is a hope they will be seen, but the very display of some items will hasten their demise. This goes against the expectation that museums look after material 'in perpetuity'. Limiting the time certain fugitive items like fabrics or watercolours are on display will lessen the damage – but it means they will not be 'out' and available to see.

Jenny Lindsaye's cape is by Egerton Burnett of Wellington, Somerset, and was worn over her uniform. It is made from grey wool flannel 'Royal serge' with scarlet lining and edged collar, and matching scarlet button holes. A metal hook and eye fastens the neck, with buttons down the front.

#084 E2018.2508

SWEETHEART BROOCH

Sweetheart brooches were tangible expressions of love between wives, mothers, siblings and girlfriends, and their loved ones who were away fighting.

Wearing something as a love token or to show you had someone special away fighting and that you were thinking about them, is not a new idea. During the First and Second World Wars, however, military jewellery became very popular, fed by jewellers who saw a gap in the market. They started to mass-produce miniature versions of items like regimental badges as brooches or pins and it was mainly soldiers who bought them for family members. Sweetheart brooches, as they became known, also served to start a conversation between wives, mothers and girlfriends about their family members who were serving, especially if information could be exchanged about those in the same unit, undergoing similar experiences.

Tokens ranged in quality and price; decorative examples could be found in gold and platinum, mounting diamonds, while cheaper versions were made of Perspex, mother-of-pearl or enamel. They could also be homemade – unit collar badges or buttons for example were re-purposed into simple brooches. Some tokens carried sentimental messages such as 'Forget me not', 'Faith, hope and charity', 'Peace, Victory and Good Luck'.

In the First World War 'Mizpah' brooches were produced in many forms. Mizpah is a Hebrew word meaning 'a watchtower' and 'here we rest'. Probably the most popular were the double hearts depicting united love with the Mizpah prayer engraved onto the hearts. 'And Mizpah; for he said, The Lord watch between me and thee, when we are absent one from another.' (Genesis 31:49) So the wearer of a Mizpah brooch may have believed or hoped that their loved one was being watched over by God.

This example of an enamelled Royal Tank Regiment brooch was given by Donald Woolnough and is pinned to his photograph. On the back of the picture is a dedication written 'To Liberty, Love Don, 31/10/44'.

Donald Woolnough pinned a Royal Tank Regiment sweetheart brooch (at top left) to his photograph taken 'somewhere in the Middle East' during 1944 and presented it to 'Liberty'.

The actual size of Donald Woolnough's enamelled Royal Tank Regiment sweetheart brooch is tiny, measuring all of 27mm high and 20mm across. It could have been worn by a loved one on a lapel or pinned to a neck scarf.

The crew of a Mark V tank inspect a captured *T-Gewehr* at the Battle of Amiens in August 1918. Both a Mark V and a *T-Gewehr* are displayed in The Tank Museum's exhibition halls.

#085 E1952.20

MAUSER 1918 T-GEWEHR

The *T-Gewehr* was as tall as a man at 5ft 6½in and weighed 41lbs. When it was fired the recoil force into the gunner's shoulder was strong enough to be painful.

The *T-Gewehr* is the first purpose-designed anti-tank weapon. Rifles to fire armour-piercing bullets were used in the frontlines before the appearance of the tank. Armoured shields were used as observation and sniper posts on the parapets of trenches. The Germans also had a 7.92mm S.m.K bullet that had a steel core and could be fired from the standard German rifle.

When the tank first appeared, the Germans used the S.m.K. and also tried reversing bullets – turning the projectile around but firing it from the same cartridge case. Fired at short ranges, the blunt end of the bullet would hit the armour first, sometimes it might penetrate but often it would distort the armour and cause 'spall' or fragments to fly off the inside surface of the tank and injure the crew. The arrival of the Mark IV tank with 12mm or ½in armour plate made it harder for the S.m.K bullet to penetrate. Other anti-tank ideas were put into service – field artillery and mines along with ditches and hidden traps, but a weapon that could be more widely issued and easily employed was needed. A 13.2mm round called TuF (for *Tank und Flieger* – tank and flyer) was being designed for a forthcoming machine-gun and it was also decided to use this in a new rifle. Elephant and punt guns provided early examples to imitate large calibre weapons to be fired by one man. Production of the bolt action, single-shot *T-Gewehr* weapon began in May 1918.

A two-man team used the *T-Gewehr*, both of whom could fire the gun. Every infantry company was due to be issued with three weapons. Some 4,632 had been issued by September 1918 and by the war's end 15,800 had been made. A bipod helped steady the long and heavy weapon but did little to lessen its considerable recoil and punch on the firer's shoulder.

The round could penetrate all the tanks then in service, but it had the problem that unless a crewmember or vital part of the vehicle was hit, the small size of the round might mean a number could be fired and penetrate a tank but no disabling shot would be achieved.

This example was captured at Vertain on 23 October 1918. These weapons seem to have been a particularly desirable souvenir for tank crews to collect.

Patriot class No 45507 *Royal Tank Corps* was built at Crewe Works in 1932 and plied the West Coast mainline with LMS and British Railways express passenger trains over three decades. It was withdrawn from service on 20 October 1962 and broken up the following year at Crewe.

#086 E1963.1.1 & E1963.1.2

ROYAL TANK CORPS LOCOMOTIVE NAMEPLATES

To mark the 20th anniversary in 1937 of the Battle of Cambrai, an LMS Patriot class express locomotive was named *Royal Tank Corps*.

In 1937, the Royal Tanks Corps had a steam locomotive named after it. The locomotive, a Patriot class of the London, Midland and Scottish Railway (LMS), was officially named at a ceremony on 20 November 1937 at Euston Station. Sir Ernest Swinton, Colonel Commandant of the Royal Tank Corps, remarked that he had 'the devil's own job to break the bottle of champagne'.

As an express passenger locomotive, *Royal Tank Corps* covered over one million miles between August 1932 and May 1962. When it was taken out of service the nameplates were presented to the regiment by British Railways. No 45507 ran in Crimson Lake livery, as seen behind the lower nameplate, but mostly wore the Brunswick Green livery shown above.

Such nameplates have become classic collectables for railway enthusiasts and are sought-after items. After years of display these nameplates were taken on by railway enthusiast Charles Reed, whose father served with the Tank Corps in 1917–18. He kindly oversaw their restoration and they are now on display in the Tank Story Hall.

London Euston Station, 20 November 1937: Sir Ernest Swinton, Colonel Commandant of the Royal Tank Corps, unveils Patriot class locomotive No 45507 *Royal Tank Corps*.

#087 E2015.4178

ESCAPE ROUTE 1940

After the German invasion, notes showing the route for the withdrawal of tanks from France were pinned to trees and tank crews had to copy and replace them – the last crews were instructed to remove them completely.

After the German breakthrough at Sedan in May 1940 and the race to the sea, the British Commander-in-Chief, General Lord John Gort, realised that to save the British Expeditionary Force (BEF) he would have to find ways his Army could retreat to the Channel ports and escape encirclement. The attack by the 4th and 7th Royal Tank Regiments created breathing space to allow the reinforcement of the garrisons at Dunkirk, Boulogne and Calais. Troops were directed to the coast but the initial expectations of how many men might be saved were not high. The rescue of the British Army and many French soldiers is the stuff of legend – over 330,000 men were evacuated via Dunkirk.

What is not often remembered is the sacrifice of troops to allow the evacuation to take place. Soldiers held Calais and further troops were landed in June with the plan that a second British Expeditionary Force might be formed, including many of the units that had not made it to Dunkirk. The 1st Armoured Division had tried to reach the troops surrounded at Dunkirk but failed. It was one of the units that were finally directed to different seaports – a further 144,000 British troops ultimately returned to Britain from other French ports.

This desperate note shows the route that one unit (perhaps from the 5th Royal Tank Regiment) was instructed to take in order to escape from France back to the UK. Presumably the last men to copy the directions took the note down and placed it in a map case or notebook and it survived their escape. The road to safety was:

1. La Hutte
2. Sillé
3. Évron
4. Montsûrs
5. Laval
6. Vitré
7. Rennes
8. St-Méen
9. Loudéac
10. Rostrenen
11. Carhaix
12. Huelgoat
13. Landerneau
14. Brest.

The collapse of the Allied armies in the face of the German advance in May 1940 led to chaos and confusion. Here the crew of a Light Mark VIB confer with a French infantryman.

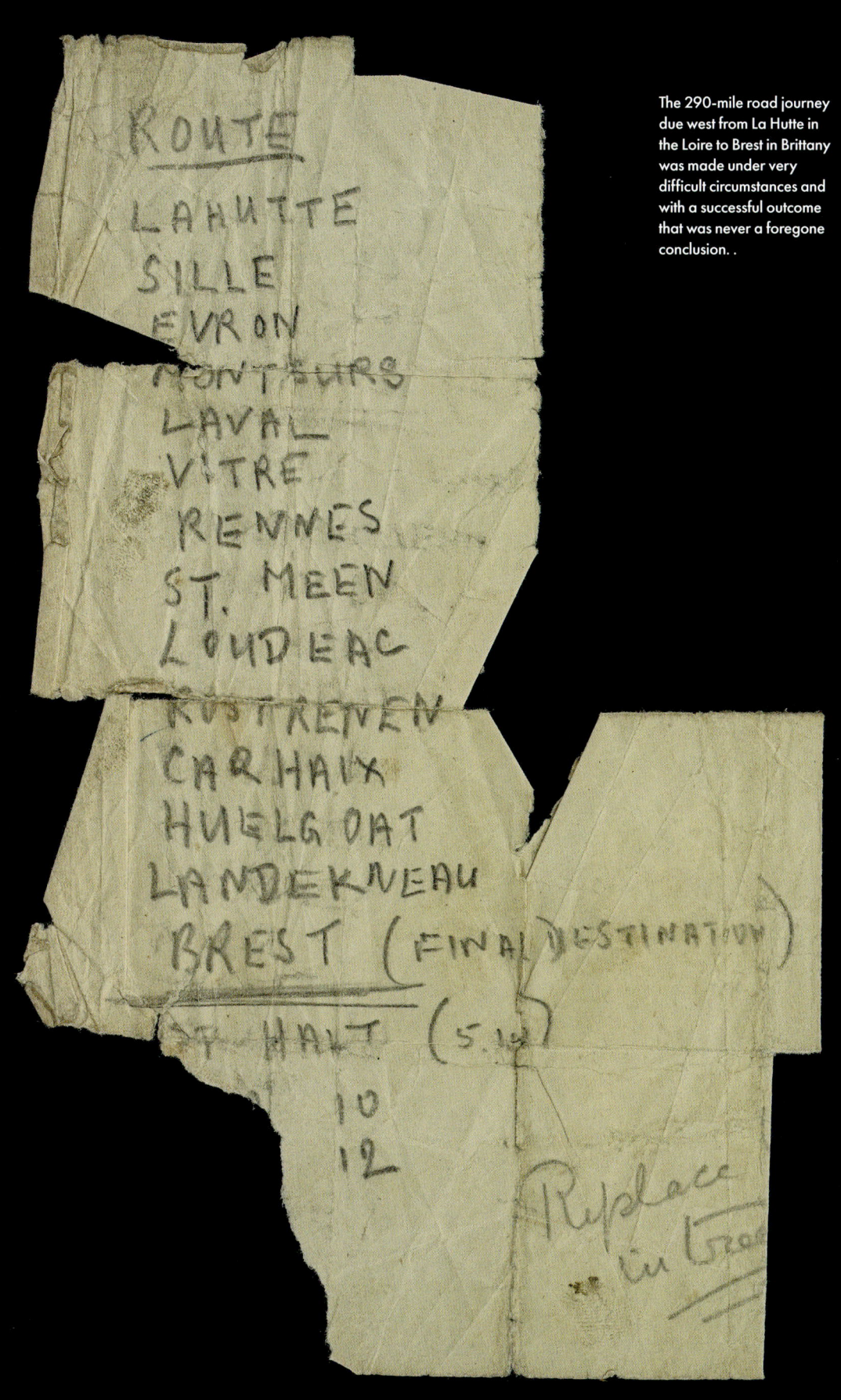

The 290-mile road journey due west from La Hutte in the Loire to Brest in Brittany was made under very difficult circumstances and with a successful outcome that was never a foregone conclusion. .

#088 E2013.422
WALTER RATCLIFFE'S UNIFORM

The 1902 Pattern SD tunic, worn here by Walter Ratcliffe, was the standard uniform of other ranks and NCOs in the British Army throughout the First World War.

This tunic was worn by Walter Ratcliffe in the First World War. Walter enlisted in 1915 and initially served in the Royal Engineers. The need for more tank crews led to men being compulsorily transferred in 1918, Ratcliffe being one of them. After three months training, he served at the Reinforcement Depot in France before being posted to the 9th Battalion the Tank Corps. In September during an engagement at Bellenglise his tank was hit. One crewmember was killed and four wounded. Ratcliffe got three of the wounded to safety and returned to stay the night with the badly wounded fourth man. The following morning, he was able to get him away safely, too. For his action Ratcliffe was awarded the Military Medal.

It is unusual to be able to display a uniform from the First World War in such good condition and even rarer to have a photograph of the owner wearing it. The brass badge on the upper left sleeve is the emblem of the 3rd French Infantry Division. It features a bursting grenade and has a special significance as in July 1918 the 9th Battalion assisted the French in a successful attack on a German position. In recognition of their support, the Division commander awarded his unit's badge to the soldiers of the 9th Battalion, Tank Corps. The lanyard was awarded to crewmen as a recognition for brave action.

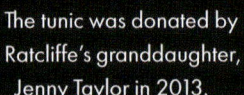

Above: Walter Ratcliffe as a corporal wearing his service dress. Note the Tank Corps embroidered cloth arm badge.

Below: Badge of the 3rd French Infantry Division (see opposite).

The tunic was donated by Ratcliffe's granddaughter, Jenny Taylor in 2013.

'I'm absolutely delighted to donate it. Just to put it back in the wardrobe seemed such a waste so I was thrilled when The Tank Museum actually said they would like to keep it. Now I know it's safe for posterity and other people can enjoy it and see it.'

Walter Ratcliffe's 1902 Pattern Service Dress (SD) tunic for Other Ranks is made from thick Khaki wool serge and was worn with webbing belt, 1902 Pattern SD trousers, and puttees wrapped around the lower leg.

#089 E1980.97.6

CLEMENT ARNOLD'S WATCH

As a token of his appreciation for saving his life, Clement Arnold gave a German officer his most prized possession, his twenty-first birthday present.

This watch was given to Clement Arnold on his 21st birthday by his father. He was wearing it on 8 August 1918 when commanding a Whippet tank called *Musical Box*. Arnold took the tank on what can only be described as a rampage among the German troops – taking on gun positions and decimating enemy troop formations assembling to attack. After being in action for over 10 hours, Arnold's crew were exhausted and petrol running into the cab from cans on the roof caught fire. The three crew bailed out: the driver, William Carnie, was shot and killed, gunner Christopher Ribbans and Arnold were attacked by German soldiers seeking revenge for the killing of so many of their comrades.

A German officer, Ritter Ernst von Maravic, intervened to stop the attack and saved their lives. Arnold showed his gratitude by giving von Maravic his watch. Ribbans and Arnold survived their imprisonment. Von Maravic and Arnold made contact again in 1931 and formed a close, unlikely friendship. Arnold visited von Maravic at Freiburg in Germany and they both laid wreaths at the town's war memorial. During one of their visits von Maravic returned the watch to Arnold.

Both were to fight again when their countries went to war in 1939.

Clement Arnold (right) and Ernst von Maravic (centre) at one of their meetings in the 1930s. Arnold was awarded the DSO for the action on 8 August 1918. He returned to service in the Second World War with the Royal Regiment of Artillery. Maravic wears the uniform of the Reichsarbeitsdienst (Reich Labour Service).

#090 E2011.2998
SCRATCH-BUILT 1/12TH SCALE KING TIGER

Dennis Downie spent four years painstakingly building this 3-foot long aluminium scale replica of a King Tiger.

In May 2011, The Tank Museum was contacted by a friend of Dennis Downie who was sadly dying. Dennis had been an avid modelmaker, mainly having built boats. In the 1990s he visited The Tank Museum on two occasions to measure the pre-production King Tiger tank.

His creation of this outstandingly detailed 1/12th-scale model took over three and a half years. Dennis had a fully-equipped machine shop, which he used for at least three hours a day during the build programme. Raw materials consisted of a 4ft x 8ft sheet of 3mm aluminium, which was used for the main framework and ribs. A 4in square-section aluminium bar was used for the wheels and tracks. Each track link was milled out to shape and size, 90 for each side. Superb attention to detail can be seen – the internal barrel diameter is 7mm, which is correct to scale for the gun.

The tank is powered by two electric motors, one for each track to allow it to be driven left or right. A further motor drives the turret and another drives the recoil on the gun's barrel.

Before Dennis died, The Tank Museum was able to arrange for the acquisition of his model and its integration into the collection as an outstanding piece of scratch-built modelmaking.

Dennis based his model on the museum's pre-production King Tiger. Here it is, photographed at Haustenbeck in Germany shortly after its capture in 1945.

#091 E2014.4589.1

AIR OBSERVATION CARDS OF THE FIRST TANK ATTACK

One of the earliest examples of tactical reconnaissance from the air took place over the battlefield at Flers-Courcelette.

```
                                              Army Form W3406.
To be delivered at once to  3rd Corps

Date 16-9-16  No. 34  Squadron, R.F.C.  Observer _____  Map

Time.    | Place.
11-15    | MARTIN ALLEY full of our men as far
         | as M33 a 46.
         | MARTIN TRENCH & THE BOW also
         | crowded with our men
         | PRUE TRENCH has no one
         | visible in it. There has been
         | no new digging in it, & the
         | parapet still faces South
                                              [OVER.]
```

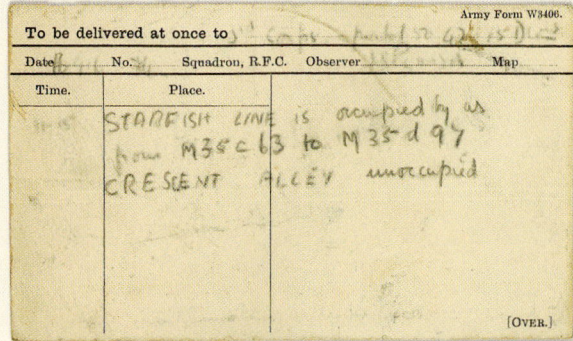

In the First World War, technology and the nature of the fighting changed rapidly. Despite the widespread myth portrayed in the 1980s BBC sitcom Blackadder, British forces under Field Marshal Haig eagerly grasped new technology as a means to help win the war and lessen British casualties.

One area where the technology seemed to lag when compared to other advances was in the field of communications. On the battlefield no effective wireless system for transmitting radio messages came into service until the war's end, and even then it was still a delicate and vulnerable affair. Telephone lines were apt to get broken under shellfire even if cables could be deployed behind advancing troops.

However, the new capabilities of aircraft and balloons allowed for observation and reporting from the air. Observers could write reports and drop them from aircraft to give up-to-date information on the progress of a battle. It called for a cool head and an element of luck as aircraft had to cross a battlefield low enough to observe the action and hopefully miss exchanges of artillery fire. These observation cards were written on 16 September 1916, the second day of the first tank attack at Flers-Courcelette, by Lieutenant Thomas Sydney Pearson MC, of 34 Squadron, Royal Flying Corps.

Pearson is credited with spotting German trenches that should have been cleared after heavy bombardment but were still full of troops. The message was received and the attack stopped, saving many lives.

Pearson served in 34 Squadron at the same time as Albert Ball VC, and he flew until the end of the war in FE2 and RE8 aircraft.

This sequence of observation cards was written from above the battlefield at Flers-Courcelette by Lieutenant Thomas Pearson in the cockpit of his 34 Squadron BE2 spotter aircraft, flying from the aerodrome at Allonville, north-east of Amiens. They span from mid-morning to mid-afternoon on 16 September 1916. Mention is made of two tanks advancing towards Eaucourt, and the German Starfish Line (*Neuer Foureaux Riegel*), with Martin Trench and Prue Trench, which were among the Second Objective on the first day of the battle, 15 September.

Opposite top: The Royal Aircraft Factory BE2 was widely employed by the RFC in frontline service from 1914 until 1917.

#092 E2014.3782

MARTEL TANK MASCOT

This unique steel and copper riveted mascot of a First World War tank took pride of place on the bonnet of General Giffard Le Quesne Martel's car.

Giffard Le Quesne Martel joined the Royal Engineers before the First World War. He was tasked with building the trench system at Elveden to be used by the first tank crews and became a great advocate for the tank, seeing it as a weapon with huge potential. Martel wrote a paper in November 1916 called 'A Tank Army' and this had an influence on J.F.C. Fuller's thinking about the tank. Martel – or 'Q' as he was known to many – served in France at the Tank Corps Headquarters alongside Fuller, helping him to plan tank operations.

After the war he was placed in charge of the Experimental Bridging Establishment at Christchurch, Hampshire, and came up with a modular box girder bridge. This was adopted by the Army and influenced the design of the famous Bailey Bridge. He also built his own one-man tank in his garage and continued showing interest in the developments of armoured forces in Britain.

Martel held senior positions with the Mechanisation Board of the Army and was placed in charge of the 50th (Northumbrian) Division, which saw action in France in 1940. He was made Director Royal Armoured Corps and later sent to Moscow as the Head of the British Military Mission. He realised the Soviet tank experience would be useful and more relevant to tank warfare after D-Day than the British desert experience.

This mascot was carried on his car and was later given to his driver J.H. Munns of the Army Service Corps – seen behind the wheel in the picture opposite. The mascot reflects the pride felt by those involved in the invention and development of the first tanks.

Opposite page: J.H. Munns behind the wheel of Martel's Sheffield Simplex car. The mascot can be seen on the bonnet.

Main images: The fine craftsmanship and attention to detail of Martel's car mascot is plain to see.

The Centurion has fought in almost all theatres of operation except that for which it was designed — North West Europe.

#093 E1970.151

CENTURION

With a diverse combat record that began in Korea in 1951 when it fired its first rounds in action, the Centurion fought its last campaign in the Gulf War of 1991.

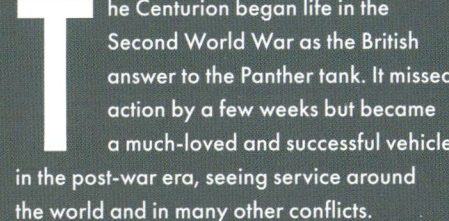

The Centurion began life in the Second World War as the British answer to the Panther tank. It missed action by a few weeks but became a much-loved and successful vehicle in the post-war era, seeing service around the world and in many other conflicts.

Powered by the Rolls-Royce Meteor engine, the Centurion had good levels of armour with a well-sloped front glacis plate and a main weapon that went through three different calibres. It was first fitted with the 17pdr, then the 20pdr on the Mark 3 version in 1948. The L7 105mm gun was fitted to the Mark 5/2 version from 1959 onwards.

The Centurion evolved through 13 marks in British service and was sold worldwide, bringing much needed currency into a struggling economy. It saw action in the Korean War, the Middle East and with Australian forces in Vietnam. It is still in service with the South African Army as the Olifant.

Seen by many as a great tank, the Centurion is arguably the best of the immediate post-war period. Some clear arguments back this reasoning: it could be improved on over time – the sign of a good basic design, it was reliable and could be worked on and fixed by the crew. But in accounts by some crewmen, there are other, less obvious reasons why the tank was held in high regard. The vehicle looked good – for many it is still the epitome of what a tank should look like. Its ability to be repaired, to somehow make it through, gave it a heart and a special identity to the crew. I have seen veterans pat the tank in a moment of reflection, mouthing thanks and affection.

#094 E1977.62

T-54 TANK

From the late 1950s the T-54 formed the core of Soviet and Warsaw Pact armoured units and was a serious threat to NATO land forces in Europe.

The Tank Museum's T-54 can be found in the Vehicle Conservation Centre. It served with the Syrian Army before being captured by the Israelis in 1967 (Six-Day War) or 1973 (Yom Kippur War), although which is uncertain. Subsequently it was passed to the British authorities and came to The Tank Museum in August 1976.

Soviet use of tanks in the Second World War gave the Red Army and its commanders a belief in the tank and artillery as the primary land weapons. Possible replacements for the T-34 were developed during the war — the T-43 and T-44 — but it was decided to continue improving the earlier vehicle instead with a new turret. This was considered a more practical evolutionary route rather than stopping factories to re-tool for a brand-new model. Work on the T-44 continued, however, and by the war's end a new prototype that would become the T-54 had been developed. It had a 'frying pan'-shaped turret of cast steel that gave good all-round ballistic protection and a well-sloped front glacis plate of 100mm. It used a development of the T-34's diesel engine and carried a 100mm main gun. The tank went into production in two main factories at the end of the 1940s.

The T-54 went through a series of improvements and a newer model, the T-55, was introduced to cope with the prospect of nuclear and chemical warfare. It was built not only for the Soviet Army but for other Warsaw Pact countries, too, and it was exported around the world. It is thought the two models are the most produced tanks of all time, with estimates of around 100,000 quoted. The tank was also built in Poland and Czechoslovakia, and a copy was made in China after the Soviet Union handed over plans and assisted in the construction of new Chinese tank factories.

The T-54 and T-55 have seen combat with many armies and insurgent forces around the world. Despite being dated, its simplicity and the sheer numbers built mean it will continue to be used for decades to come.

#095 E1991.111.2
VICKERS TANK PERISCOPE MARK IV

Patented in 1936 by Polish engineer Rudolf Gundlach, the Vickers Tank Periscope Mark IV was the first device to allow a tank commander a 360-degree view from inside his turret using a single periscope.

A constant problem for tank crews is seeing what is going on around them, especially when a vehicle is 'buttoned-up' with the hatches closed. In the first tanks a thin, tubular, handheld periscope was raised through the roof of the front cab to allow the commander or driver to look outside. This was supplemented by small oblong vision ports cut into the armour plate that had a metal housing behind to hold two angled, polished metal plates. These acted as mirrors to allow the crew to look outside the vehicle without having to directly expose their eyes to any incoming fire or shell splinters.

The use of glass periscopes was widespread before the Second World War but they had disadvantages. Unless mounted in a rotating housing they could only look one way, and even then a crewman would not always be able to position himself to turn 360 degrees and look out of the periscope. This problem was addressed by the Polish engineer, Rudolf Gundlach. He held the rank of major in the Polish Corps of Engineers and headed its Armoured Weapons Development Office. Gundlach created a periscope where the viewer could use an upper vision port to see forwards or a fold-down lower vision port that allowed them to see rearwards. The design, first used in 1935 in Polish tanks like the TKS and 7TP, was patented in 1936.

With war approaching and as part of a package of Polish-British cooperative military ventures, the designs for the scope were sold to Vickers for a token sum of one zloty. In Britain, the design became known as the Vickers Tank Periscope Mark IV and it was fitted to nearly all British tanks from 1940. The idea was also copied by German and Soviet forces.

Gundlach escaped to France with many thousands of other Polish troops in 1939, but ill health meant he spent the rest of the war in Vichy France. After the war, he was awarded money for his invention by both France and Britain, and he bought a bakery outside Paris that became a meeting place for Polish emigrés.

The Vickers Tank Periscope Mark IV was fitted with two vision ports. By rotating the periscope through 180 degrees a tank commander was able to look backwards through the second eyepiece, meaning he no longer had to change position to look behind the turret.

#096

E1983.309, E1951.5, E1949.398, E1949.396, E1954.43, E1949.389, E1952.24, E1951.3, E1949.399, E1949.397, E1949.393, E1949.394, E1949.392

THE GUN BARREL DISPLAY

Combining firepower, strong armour and battlefield mobility, the ultimate expression of a tank's strength is its gun.

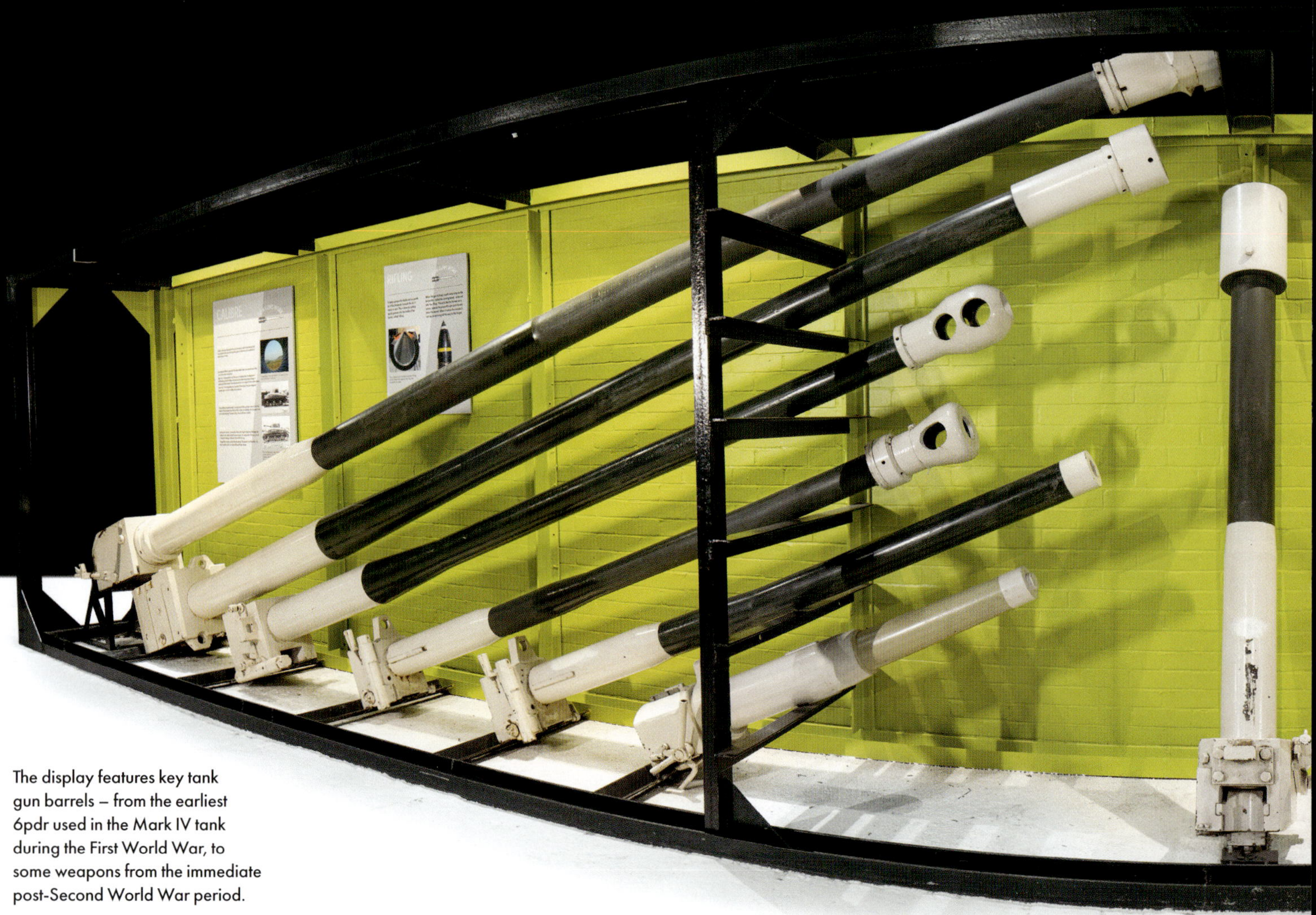

The display features key tank gun barrels — from the earliest 6pdr used in the Mark IV tank during the First World War, to some weapons from the immediate post-Second World War period.

This arrangement of gun barrels has been on display at The Tank Museum for decades. In earlier days, there were examples of secondary armament – machine guns – welded to the top rail. With changing attitudes to conservation and gun legislation, however, these guns were removed in the 1980s.

The angled barrels create a decorative look and build on a tradition of cannon and barrels being used as part of an architectural motif. Barrels that failed to Proof (meaning they were not safe to use) and captured French ship cannons were used as road bollards in London. Some of these remain to this day and bollards are still made imitating this style. Cannons were also carved in stone to form bases and in architectural pediments for sculptures and on buildings.

As well as looking impressive, the barrel display charts progress of main armament on tanks.

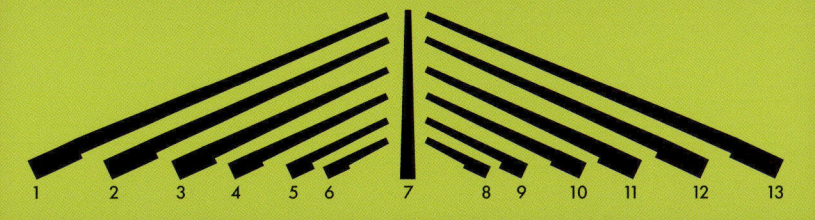

1 Ordnance QF 32pdr, **2** Ordnance QF 20pdr, **3** Ordnance QF 77mm, **4** Ordnance QF 75mm, **5** Ordnance QF 6pdr 7cwt, **6** Ordnance QF 6cwt Hotchkiss Mark I, **7** Ordnance QF 95mm Close Support Howitzer, **8** Ordnance QF 3.7" Close Support Mortar **9** Ordnance QF 2pdr, **10** 37mm M6, **11** 75mm M3, **12** Ordnance QF 17pdr, **13** 8.8cm KampfwagenKanone 43.

They date from the first 6pdr (or 57mm) guns for the Mark IV, through other key tank barrels, mainly British, from the Second World War and the immediate postwar period. Space ran out, so a newer display of more modern tank barrels is now on show in the Tank Story hall.

When a recent refurbishment of the Second World War gallery was carried out the removal of the barrel display was debated. Ultimately it was retained because it illustrates the rapid increase in tank gun sizes and because it is a museum 'fixture' that many returning visitors will remember.

#097 E1951.21
STURMGESCHÜTZ

When fitted with the lethal 7.5cm StuK 40 L/48 gun, the *Sturmgeschütz* (or *StuG*) was capable of engaging and defeating almost all Allied armour at long range, claiming many kills.

Second World War German tanks like the Tiger and Panther get the attention in most histories. This is certainly the case with modelmakers and gameplayers — but it was actually the clever use of the *Sturmgeschütz* that caused most Allied tank casualties in the North West Europe campaign. A postwar operational report stated tank losses were due to:

24.4 per cent to self-propelled guns
22.7 per cent to anti-tank guns
22.1 per cent to mines
14.5 per cent to tanks
14.2 per cent to hand-held anti-tank weapons (such as the *Panzerfaust*).

As the German military theorised in the 1930s over how tanks might be used in future warfare, Heinz Guderian argued strongly for the use of Panzer divisions — a concentrated tank force, rather than spreading tanks out among the infantry. Colonel Erich von Manstein, a forward-thinker himself, argued that some form of mobile armour was also needed to escort the infantry into battle, and he pushed for the development of the *Sturmgeschütz* or assault gun. The gun would accompany infantry on the attack to fire at pill-boxes and machine-gun emplacements and potentially enemy tanks if they were to appear. The Panzer divisions following behind with their tanks could use their speed and mobility to exploit any breakthrough.

The first *Sturmgeschütz* vehicles carried a short-barrelled 75mm gun fitted into a casemate, not a turret, on a Panzer III chassis. This lack of the turret made the vehicle's profile low and, in consequence, a harder target for defenders to hit. The vehicles were manned by artillery crews and allocated to infantry units.

As the war progressed, tank fighting grew in importance as a key component of land warfare. Hitler was instrumental in approving the addition of longer barrelled, higher velocity anti-tank guns to the *Sturmgeschütz*, which resulted in the vehicle's role changing. It was now to act in a predominantly anti-tank capacity. Simpler and cheaper to build than a turreted tank (three *Sturmgeschütz* could be built for the price of two Panzer III tanks), the low profile of the vehicle made it an ideal ambush and defensive weapon — and Germany was on the defensive from mid-1943.

The history of this *Sturmgeschütz Ausf G* model is currently unknown but it retains much of its original *Zimmerit* or anti-magnetic paste. This was a coating applied by German factories from autumn 1943 to create a barrier to stop magnetic mines adhering to the metal of the tank. As the Allies did not use any form of magnetic mine, the Germans dropped the practice in September 1944.

#098 E2011.4892

WIRELESS SET No 19

The Wireless Set No 19 was the British Army's most widely used radio of the Second World War, remaining in active service until the 1960s.

Communication between tanks and other military units is essential for success on the battlefield. The early use of carrier pigeons, flags and semaphore led to some experiments with radio before the end of 1918. However, the glass valves in the early radios were very vulnerable to damage. Between the wars, British experiments on Salisbury Plain with crystal radio sets showed how a force could be effectively led by one voice. For speed and control the radio was now deemed essential, but not all armies could acquire enough of them. Therefore, for so many, flag control remained in use during the early years of the Second World War.

Designed in 1940 by the Experimental Signals Establishment and the Pye Radio Company, the No 19 Set replaced the earlier No 11 Set in British tanks and many other vehicles. Improvements led to a Mark II and Mark III model. Examples were also built in Canada where Russian and English instructional writing was added to the front. This was because the radios were built as part of the Lend-Lease arrangements and some would be sent to the Soviet Union.

The No 19 Set could be used in several ways: it had an intercom (or IC) for the crew to talk to each other; the driver had a control box with a buzzer to attract the commander's attention if he was busy on another channel; the B Set allowed communication between the other tanks of the troop; and the A Set, communication at longer range – to Regimental Headquarters, for example. Usually, the two external channels were mixed onto the internal IC channel so the crew could hear what was going on. There were the inevitable embarrassing mistakes when crews thought they were on the IC, but instead broadcast to the rest of the squadron or higher formations.

Radio etiquette was important to maintain in action and the calming voice of a commander could bring reassurance and order to the immediate chaos of battle. Jock Watt fought in the 3rd Royal Tank Regiment under the command of 'Pip' Roberts: 'A man who had commanded discipline and respect like no other I had served under. His calm voice on the radio with comments such as, "come on now don't be shy, get up into line with me," reduced the most frightening situation to a tolerable level.'

Above: The Wireless Set No 19 weighed in at 40lbs. The dial on the right is the main transceiver tuning control and on the left the tuning for the 807 power amplifier. In the centre of each dial is a square 'knob' used for pre-setting frequencies to make it easier for the radio operator in the tank to maintain his place in a net when the tank was in action.

Left: Not all armies could get hold of enough radios in 1939 and they had to rely on flag control during the early years of the Second World War.

THE TANK MUSEUM IN 100 OBJECTS 201

#099 E2014.2596

JOHNSON 'SNAKE' TRACK

A cable fitted with track plates capable of free lateral movement was tested on a Mark V tank, which made it drive faster, but the idea was abandoned as it had no official support.

In the First World War, after the introduction of the faster Whippet tank (or Medium A), a series of designs for Medium tanks was developed. The Medium B was followed shortly by the Medium C or 'Hornet'. These were to be tanks of exploitation – needing range and speed if they were to follow Tank Corps theorist J.F.C. Fuller's idea for deep and rapid tank advances, for his 'Plan 1919'. The war ended before any of these ideas could be acted on in the way Fuller envisaged, although the use of combined arms and faster vehicles like armoured cars did show great progress at the Battle of Amiens in August 1918.

Lieutenant Colonel Phillip Johnson was an engineer at one of the tank workshops in France in 1918. He experimented with making existing tanks faster and came up with what became known as 'snake' track. This was a cable fitted with track plates that had free lateral movement. The track was trialled on a Mark V tank, which reached the incredible speed of 20mph compared to the usual 4mph.

Johnson added a new suspension system based on a cable that threaded through pulleys mounted on the roadwheels and the tank's hull. The sprung effect provided the vehicle with more speed and mobility. Despite the end of the war, Winston Churchill, as Minister of Supply, was able to ensure Johnson could carry on with his experiments to produce a new, amphibious tank called the Medium D. The tank had the new suspension and steering based on the flexibility of the track, which could be bowed to allow a change in the vehicle's direction.

Despite its technical advantages the Medium D had many problems. When Churchill left the Ministry, the project lacked enough support and Johnson's department was closed down in 1923. This section of snake track actually comes from another Johnson project – a proposed Light infantry tank from 1921.

Left: A Mark V trialling Johnson's snake track.

Above: Phillip Johnson in later life.

Main picture: This section of snake track is all that remains of Johnson's ideas as there are no surviving Medium D tanks.

#100 E2022.579
MARK I BLUEPRINT

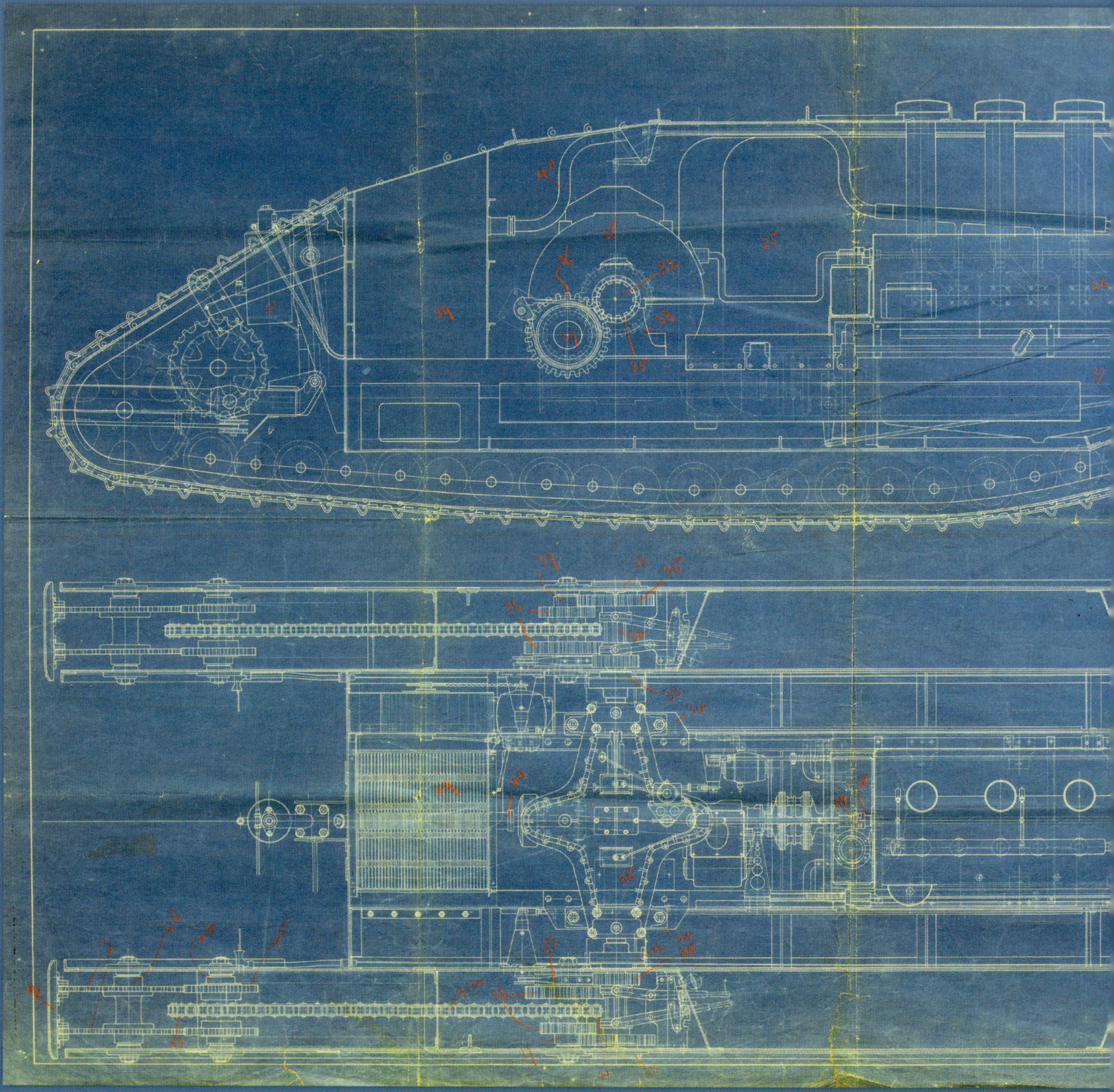

William Tritton – looking the archetypal Edwardian engineer – was the Managing Director of William Foster & Co, the builders of 'Little Willie' and 'Mother'.

Thanks to the financial support of a former Royal Tank Regiment officer, The Tank Museum successfuly bid for and won this rare piece of tank history at auction.

It is amazing what interesting items can still be found relating to the early history of the tank. This blueprint of a First World War tank, dated 18 May 1916, shows features of development from 'Mother', the prototype, but with differences to the actual production Mark I tanks. It was found in an attic along with a draft patent for the new tank that was never actually submitted. The two items were put up for auction with a fanfare of publicity by the auctioneers in 2022. It is the earliest blueprint of the tank known to exist.

Blueprints were a way of making multiple copies of line drawings for use by manufacturers. Light sensitive paper was laid against the original black-lined drawing and exposed to light. This led to the reproduction of a drawing with white lines on a blue background. The process leaves a fugitive image – one that is still sensitive to light over time.

The Tank Museum holds several original line drawings for Mark I tanks, but only has blueprints for later models of First World War tanks, so this item and the patent document were of obvious interest for the Archive. Fortunately, the publicity surrounding the sale brought forward a potential backer, a former Royal Tank Regiment officer named Tim Allan, who offered financial support, allowing the museum to bid at auction.

As part of the due diligence process, an expert on First World War tank production looked at the drawing on behalf of the museum to verify its condition and authenticity. The museum was then able to secure the item at the auction, bidding by telephone. Another important piece of tank history has now been acquired for public benefit.

INDEX

Action Man Scorpion Tank 142-3
Admiralty, The 6
Admiralty Air Department 63
Afghanistan 24-5
Ager, Norman 82-3
Air Board 61
Alam Halfa, Battle of 39
Aldridge, Buzz 122
Allan, Tim 205
Amatol 150
Ambidge, Lt Col 47
Amiens, Battle of 36, 110-1, 174, 202
Ammunition:
  Anti-tank (AT) 80; Armour-piercing (AP) 138; Armour Piercing Capped (APC) 138; Armour Piercing Capped Ballistic Capped (APCBC) 138; Armour Piercing Discarding Sabot (APDS) 138-9; Case shot 111; 0.303in 73; .455 133; 13.2mm TuF 175; Cartridges, rimmed and rimless 73; High Explosive (HE) 111; Hollow charge 80, 81, 96, 137; 7.92mm 73, 115; 7.92mm S.m.K. 175
An Onlooker in France 1917–1919 (book) 164
Arab Revolt 1917 63
Armour 81
Armour plate 13, 97, 175, 193
Armoured Odyssey (book) 42, 107
Armstrong Whitworth 18
Army Staff College, Camberley 160
Arnold, Clement 182-3
Arras, Battle of (1917) 57
Arras, Battle of (1940) 45
Auchinleck, Gen Claude 38
Audrey (girlfriend) 34-5
Australian forces 191
Awards and medals:
  Defence Medal 88; Distinguished Service Order 121, 183; France and Germany Star 88; Military Cross 17, 110, 111, 129; Military Medal 180; 1939-1945 Star 88; 1939-1945 War Medal 88; Victoria Cross 26-7, 81, 129
Ayer, David 122

Bailey Bridge 189
Bairnsfather, Bruce 70, 107
Baker, Lt Albert 128-9
Ball, Albert VC 187
Bayeux, France 117
Beaucamp, France 127
Beaverbrook, Lord 145, 159
Bellamy, Lt Bill 34-5
Bellenglise, France 180
'Benghazi boilers' 29
Bergen-Belsen 48-9
Berlin 47
Bermicourt, France 160, 164
Birmingham Small Arms Co (BSA) 73
Bisley 81
Black beret (Royal Tank Regiment) 38, 166-7
Black Drill, Working Dress (SP 1935) 152-3
Black uniforms 76
Blackadder, TV series 187
Blacker, Lt Col Lathan Valentine Stewart 80
Blitzkrieg 155
Board of Ordnance 74
Bocage (Normandy) 35
Boiling Vessel 28-9
Bone dome (AFV-73 helmet) 30
Book of Common Prayer 36
Bouchoir CWGC cemetery 36
Boulogne, France 178
Bovington Camp 41, 63, 111
Boyson, Gnr George 36
Bradford, Roland Boys 129
Brangwyn, Sir Frank 33
Bretteville-sur-Laize, France 88
Bridge Works, Shoreham 21
Bristol Tank Week 1917 124

British Army 17, 18, 19, 65, 100, 145, 152, 178, 200. Armies: First 38; Eighth 38, 39. Divisions: 1st Armoured 178; 7th Armoured 67; 11th Armoured 11, 48, 130-1; 50th Northumbrian 189; 51st Highland 99; 79th Armoured 49, 99. Corps: XXX 99. Brigades: 7th Armoured Brigade 17. Regiments and Corps: Armoured Car Squadron 63; Army Service Corps 189; King's Royal Irish Hussars 34; Machine Gun Corps 9, 53, 84; Heavy Branch 160; Manchester Regiment 26; Queen's Royal Irish Hussars 51; QAIMNS 170-1; Royal Armoured Corps 34, 73, 76, 88,189; 144th Regiment 88-9; Royal Engineers 127, 189; Royal Tank Corps 17, 58, 65, 76, 89, 107, 149, 152-3, 166-7, 176-7; 5th Battalion 148; Royal Tank Regiment 17, 38, 39, 45, 126, 143, 153, 166-7, 169, 172-3, 205; 1 RTR 17, 47, 116-7; 2 RTR 24; 3 RTR 200; 4 RTR 30, 152; 5 RTR 82, 84, 148-9, 178; 6 RTR 67, 83; 7 RTR 178; 8 RTR 42, 106-7; Staffordshire Yeomanry 49; Tank Corps 26, 33, 127, 128-9, 133, 146, 160, 164, 189; A Battalion 36; Field Battalion 133; H Battalion 33, 127; 2nd Battalion 134; 4th Battalion 111; 5th Armoured Company 63; 7th Battalion 128; 8th Battalion 111; 9th Battalion 180; 13th/18th Hussars 49; 49th Armoured Personnel Carrier Regiment 99; 49th General Field Hospital 170; Westminster Dragoons 11, 92

British Empire 33
British Expeditionary Force (1940) 38, 153, 178
British Military Mission, Moscow 189
British Tank Mission, Washington 105
British Timken Ltd 105
British Union of Fascists 160
BRIXMIS 102-3
Brodie helmet 53
Bullet splash 14
Bullock Creeping Grip Co, USA 41
Burroughs, LCpl R. 45
Bursting charge 13
Burton Park, Lincoln 6
Butcher, Lt Charles Edward 112
Butlins Holiday Camp 70
Butt, Capt Arthur 42
Butt, Maj Peter 42

Cairo, Egypt 117
Calais, France 178
Callwood, Amy 88-9
Callwood, Cpl Charles 88-9
Callwood, Joan 88-9
Cambrai, Battle of 26, 33, 126, 127, 128-9, 134-5, 160, 177
Cambridge University 21
Camouflage 60, 119-20
Canada 98, 109, 200
Canadian Army 99
  II Canadian Corps 99; 1st Canadian Armoured Carrier Regiment 99
Carnie, William 183
Carruthers, Pte Walter 132-3
Carver, Field Marshal Lord 16-7
Cassel, France 127
Cassino, Battle of 167
Cheshire Constabulary 133
Chief of the Defence Staff 17
Chimpanzee Valley 57
China 193
Chobham, RAF station 87
Christie, Cyril William 146
Christie, Walter 91
Christmas, Pte Thomas 36
Churchill, Winston S. 11, 38, 41, 57, 68, 203
Città Sant'Angelo 42
Cold War 102, 162
Combat Vehicle Crewman's Helmet (CVCH) 30-1
Compass Dept, Ditton Park 45

Cooper, Alfred Duff 169
Coppock, S.W. 138
Crawler track 79
Crème de Menthe, china Mk I tank 121
Crewe Works 176
Crowley, Aleistair 160
Cunliffe, Lt Marcus 88-9
Czechoslovakia 193

d'Eyncourt, Sir Eustace Tennyson 100
D-Day 22, 34, 78, 140-1,170, 189
Dagenham (Ford) 70-1
Daily Mirror 121
De Courcey, Lt Thomas Joseph 111
Defence Intelligence 102
Defence Science and Technology Laboratory 25
Denaro, Lt Col Arthur 51
Derringer-type pistol 53
Desert war 29
Detmold 47
Dewar, Michael 105
Dillon, Col Norman Margrave 134-5
Dimbleby, Richard 48
Dinky Toys 58
Dobson, Rfm Joseph William 112
Downie, Dennis 184-5
Doyle, Lt Col Paddy 148
Dunkirk, France 178

East Germany 102-3
Easter Rising 1916 63
Edgar Brandt Company 138
Egerton Burnett (uniform manufacturer) 171
Egypt 38, 63
Eisenhower, General Dwight D. 38
El Alamein, Battle of 39, 82, 83, 107
Elles, Lt Gen Hugh 126-7, 160, 164, 166
Elveden training area 109, 189
Engines: Armstrong Siddeley V8 18; Armstrong Siddeley 90hp 65; Chrysler multibank 92; Daimler Foster 105hp 21; Daimler-Knight 41; Liberty 340/410hp 91, 159; Liberty V12 27-litre 90; Rolls Royce Merlin 158-9; Rolls-Royce Meteor 91, 158-9, 191 Wright Continental 92
Estrées, France 111
Euston Station, London 177
Exercise 'Dracula' 77
Experimental Bridging Establishment 189
Experimental Mechanised Force 18, 160
Experimental Signals Establishment 200

'Fancy work' 146
Far East 17, 156
Featherstone, Sgt Donald 167
Fernie, Maj Stewart 45
Field Marshal's baton 16-17
Field Service Cap 167
Fighting Vehicles Proving Establishment (FVPE) 87
First World War 13, 21, 33, 41, 44, 47, 53, 61, 65, 81, 84, 91, 99, 100, 109, 110, 121, 146, 160, 169, 172, 180, 188, 189, 196, 205
Flers-Courcelette, Battle of 8, 112-3, 186-7
Flimsies 22, 29
Ford Motor Co 70-1, 91
Fort Halstead, Kent 137, 138
Foster, William & Co, Lincoln 6, 41, 109, 205
France 9, 21
  3rd French Infantry Division 180
Fraser, Sgt Jock 39
Freiston, Lincs 121
French Army 155
Frost, Brian 122
Fuller, Lt Col J.F.C. 127, 160-1, 189, 202
Fuller, Leonard John 84
Fury, film 68, 122-3

Gaza, Battle of 57
German Spring Offensive 1918 124
German Army 26, 96
  504th Heavy Tank Battalion 68
Germany 22
GI Joe 143
Gold-plated Challenger 1 50-1

Goodwood, Operation 116
Goring, Reichsmarschall Hermann 46-7
Gort, Gen Lord John 178
Gothic Line 42
Graincourt, France 128-9
Graincourt gun 128-9
Gran Chaco War 18
Great Patriotic War 162
'Great Swan', the 131, 159
Grünvogel, Vinzenz 22
Guderian, Gen Heinz 199
Gulf Wars 137
  1st Gulf War 29, 31, 51, 191
Gundlach, Rudolf 194

Guns and hand-held weapons:
  al Nasirah AT grenade 137; Baby Bombard 81; Bazooka 137; Blacker Bombard 81; BESA machine-gun 72-3; Boys Anti-tank Rifle 81, 145; Bren gun 72, 145; F-34 76.2mm 162; 2pdr 13, 41, 94-5, 101; 3pdr 65; 6pdr 6, 13, 57, 111; 7.7cm Feldkanone 96 n.A 129; 17pdr 13, 100, 138-9, 191; 20pdr 58, 191; 25pdr 99; 37mm 156; 37mm M6 197; 47mm 18; 75mm 101, 156; 75mm M2 105; 75mm M3 197; 75mm short-barrelled 199; 7.5cm StuK 40 L/48 198; 85mm 162; 8.8cm Kampfwagenkanone 43 197; 100mm 193; 105mm 99, 191; .50-calibre 74; Hotchkiss machine-gun 65, 111; Hotchkiss Mk I 197; Lee Enfield .303in 25; Mauser T-Gewehr 174-5; M3 105; MG 34 114-5; Ordnance QF 3.7in Close Support Mortar 197; Ordnance QF 2pdr 197; Ordnance QF 6pdr 7 cwt 197; Ordnance 17pdr 197; Ordnance QF 20pdr 197; Ordnance QF 75mm 197; Ordnance QF 77mm 197; Panzerfaust 96-7, 136, 137, 199; PIAT 80-1; QF 32pdr 197; RPG-7 AT grenade 136-7; RTG 38 150; RW 61 mortar 150; Vickers K 145; Vickers 0.303in 18, 63; Webley Mk VI .455 revolver 132-3; ZB 26 machine-gun 73; ZB 53 machine gun 73.
Gurtsack 115

Haig, Gen Douglas 57, 187
Hamburg, Germany 117
Hamilton, Capt Stuart 42, 106-7
Harding, Lt Thomas Roland 111
Hardress-Lloyd, Lt Col John 127
Harrison, Lt Col Stephen 102
Harrow School 8
Hasbro Toy Co 143
Hassall, John 108-9
Hastings, Sussex 145
Hawker Hurricane 45
Henschel factory, Kassel 68
Henriques, Lt Basil 8-9, 109
Henriques, Rose 8-9
Hepworth, Barbara 84
Heritage Lottery Fund 68, 122
Hetherington, Maj 6
Hewison, William 'Bill' 116-7
Hill, Adrian 92
Hill, E.C. 39
HM, King George V 26
HM, King George VI 78
HM, Queen Elizabeth II 16, 17, 63
HRH, The Duke of Kent 78
Hitchcock, Theordore Charles Basil 92
Hitler, Adolf 55, 150, 160, 199
Hitler Youth 97
Hobart, Maj Gen Percy 10-11, 49
Holek, Václav 73
Holland 34
Home Guard 11, 81, 145
Hornby, Frank 58
Hornsey School of Art 92
Horrocks, Lt Gen Brian 99
Horse Guards Parade, London 105
Hotblack, Maj Elliott 164
Huggins, Ron 122
Huntbach, Maj Gerald 127

India	63, 65	Brigade	112
Inglis, Capt Arthur	121	Newcastle	18
Iran	50-51	Newton, Chambers (Sheffield)	78
Italy	148	Nicholson, Ben	84
Iveagh, Lord	33	Nixon, Capt Graeme	112
		Noakes, Michael	17
Jefferis, Maj Millis	81	Norman Productions	122
Jenkin, Dvr Arthur	14	Normandy (1944)	17, 34, 77, 81, 99, 116, 131, 159, 170
Jerry can	22-3	Norway (1940)	164
Johnson, Col Phillip	202-3	North Africa	22, 23, 29, 34, 76, 82, 106, 149, 154-5, 156
Johnson 'snake' track	202-3	North West Europe	34, 77, 92
Johnston, Sgt W.L.H.	158	North West Frontier	65, 81
Jones, Lt Eddie	78	NP Aerospace	25
Jones, Mavis	78	Nuremberg War Trials	49
Jolly, Lt Col Alan	88-9	Nye, LCpl Charles	52-3
Jordan	51		
Jungle Tank Suit	77	Official War Artists	11, 33, 92, 164
		'Old Bill' cartoons	70, 108
Kennedy, Cpl Stephen	66-7	Operation Torch	38
Kennington, Eric	10-11	Orpen, Sir William	164-5
Kippspiegel-Zielfernrohr gun sight	55	Oversuit (Tank Crews)	76-7
Kladow, Germany	47	Oxford University	8
Korean War	191		
Koshkin, Mikhail	162	Palestine	83
Krupp, Essen	55	Palitoy	143
Kugelblende	115	Panzermantel für MG 34	115
Kugelzielfernrohr 2	115	Panzertruppen	167
		Patriot class locomotive No 45507	177
Lambeth School of Art	70	Royal Tank Corps	176-7
Landing Craft, Tank (LCT)	140-1	Pattern washers	74
Landships Committee	41	Pearl Harbor	10, 22
Lawrence, T.E.	11, 63	Pearson, Lt Sydney Thomas	187
Le Creusot, France	156	Perham Down	148
Lend-Lease	104-5, 200	Permutter, Monsieur L.	138
Liberty engine	91-2	P6 compass	44-5
Liddell Hart, Basil	160	Pixie suit	77
Lima Locomotive Works, USA	105	Plugging	94
Lincoln	40	Poland	193
Lincoln Cathedral	6	Porsche	55
Lindsaye, Capt Jenny	170	Prideaux speed loader	133
Little Audrey, Abbess of Chantry	34	Pritchard, Sgt Bill	34
LMS Railway	176-7	Projectile	13
Longcross Film Studios	87	*Punch* magazine	61, 116-7
London	9, 53, 61, 63	Purchasing Commission (UK)	105
Lord Mayor's Parade, London	124	Pye Radio Co	200
Lulworth, Dorset	76	Pym, Harold A.	65
Lüneburg Heath, Germany	131		
		Radium	44, 45
Macpherson, George	6	RARDE, Chertsey	86-7, 150
Manchester Pals	111	Ratcliffe, Cpl Walter	180-1
Manstein, Col Erich von	199	Red Army	55, 155, 162
Maravic, Ritter Ernst von	183	Red Cross hospital, Rouen	9
Mark 7 Combat Helmet	24-5	Reed, Charles	177
Market Garden, Operation	131	Regent Street Polytechnic, London	117
McGregor, Malcolm	66-7	Reichsarbeitsdienst (RAD)	183
McKie, Douglas	70	Rhine crossing, 1945	131
McKie, Helen	70	Ribbans, Christopher	183
Marshall, Cpl Keith	102	Ribecourt, France	33, 127
Martel, Gen Giffard Le Quesne	188-9	Ricardo, Harry	21, 100
Messines, Battle of	112	RMA Sandhurst	109
Middle East	50, 63, 83, 137, 191	Roberts, Maj Gen Pip	131, 200
Milligan, Trooper	30	Robertson, Clement VC	27
Ministry of Defence	74	Robinson, Sub-Lt Tony	141
Ministry of Information	70	Rolled homogenous armour	13
Ministry of Supply	156, 159, 203	Rolls-Royce	
Mizpah brooches	172	Clan Works, Belper 159; Silver Ghost 63	
Mond, Sir Alfred	61	Rommel, Field Marshal Erwin	38
Monroe/Neumann effect	97	Roosevelt, President Franklin D.	105
Montagu, Lord, of Beaulieu	61	Rowbotham, William	159
Montgomery, Gen B.L. (Monty)	38-9, 66, 67	Royal Academy of Arts, London	33, 84, 92, 109
Moody, Charles	92	Royal Air Force	145
Moore, Maj Humphrey	11	152 Squadron	158
Moscow	55	Royal Aircraft Factory BE2	187
Mosley, Sir Oswald	160	Royal Armouries, Leeds	74
Mostyn, Marjorie	84	Royal Flying Corps	21, 81, 187
M3 motorway	86	34 Squadron	187
Murfitt, LCpl Craig	24-5	Royal Gallery, Westminster Palace	33
Munns, Dvr J.H.	189	Royal Naval Air Service	6, 41, 63
		Royal Navy	63, 105
National Museum of Wales	33	Royal Small Arms Factory	73, 74
National War Savings Committee	124	Russia	18, 55
NATO	17, 192		
Netley Abbey Military Hospital	53	St Ives School of Painting	84
Neutrality Acts (US)	105	St Sylvain, Normandy	88
New Zealand	112		
2nd Bn, 3rd New Zealand Rifle			

Saunders, Hilary St G.	70	50-1; Shir 2 50-1; Standard Beaverette 144-5; Sturmgeschutz (StuG) 198-9; Sturmtiger 150-1; Tiger I 68, 138, 150, 199; Tiger 131 68-9, 122; T-26 18; T-34 55, 68, 162-3, 193; T-44 193; T-54 192-3; T-55 193, 194; TKS 194; TOG I 101; TOG II 100-1; TOG II* 101; Universal Carrier 70-1; Valentine 140, 156; Vickers Medium Mk II 64-5, 148; Vickers Type A 18; Vickers Type B 18; Vickers 6-ton Export 18-9; Warthog 24; Whippet (Medium A) 183, 202	
Salisbury, Lord	57		
Salisbury Plain	18, 200		
Salute the Soldier	65		
Schutzmütze	167		
Second World War	29, 47, 65, 70, 96, 99, 107, 114, 119, 122, 138, 148, 153, 159, 160, 162, 164, 167, 169, 172, 191, 194, 196, 200		
Sedan, France	178		
Seidensticker, Maj August	68		
Selfridge's, London	70		
Service Dress, 1902 Pattern	180-1	*Tanks and Tank Folk* (book)	11
Sewell, Cecil VC	27	Tea drinking	29
Shah of Iran	50, 87	Test plate	12-3
Sheffield Simplex car	189	Third Reich	46
Sherman tank 'Michael'	104-5	Trafalgar Square Tank Bank	124
Simmonds, Lt Gen Guy	99	Trafford Park, Manchester (Ford)	70
Six-Day War 1967	193	Tobruk	83
Smith, Archie (Henry)	36	TOG (The Old Gang)	100
Smith, Lilah	36	Travis, Kenneth	117
Solandt, Dr Omond McKillop	76	Treibsatz 4581 rocket motor	150
Solomon, Solomon J.	61, 109	Tripoli	82
Somme, Battle of the	57	Tritton family	6
Somme, river	45	Tritton, Sir William	6, 41, 101, 205
South African Army	191	*Troop Leader* (book)	34
South Shields School of Art	116	Tudor-Hart, Percyval	60
Soviet Army	193	Tunisia	68, 81
Soviet Union	102, 137, 162, 192, 200		
Spalling 14		Universal battledress	153
Special Vehicle Development Committee	100	US tank crews	29
Special Works (Camouflage) School	61	Usher Art Gallery, Lincoln	109
Speer, Albert	55		
Splinter mask	14-5	Vaux, 2Lt Peter	45
Stalingrad	150	Vehicle Conservation Centre, Tank Museum	193
Standard Beaverette	144-5	Vichy France	194
Stasi	102	Vickers	18, 50
Stern, Sir Albert	6, 100	Tank Periscope Mk IV	194-5
Supermarine Spitfire	45, 158-9, 162	Vietnam War	191
Swastika flag	131-2	Volkssturm	97
Sweetheart brooch	172-3		
Swinton, Sir Ernest	100, 177	Wain, Capt Richard	26-27
Sword Beach	78	War Artist Advisory Committee	11
Syrian Army	193	War Bonds	33, 124
		War Horse film	87
Taliban	24-5	War Office	9, 18, 21, 38, 60, 61, 65, 73, 101
Tamiya Hall	101	Wardrop, Jake	148-9
Tank & Tracked Transport Experiment Establishment (TTTEE)	87	Warmwell, RAF station	158
Tank Board	156	Warsaw Pact	162, 192
Tank Design Department	18	Webb, Harry	122
Tank Week	124	West, Richard VC	27
Tanks and armoured fighting vehicles: Archer 13; Beaverette Mk IV 144-5; Bergepanther 150; 'Big Willie' 6, 41; BMP 2 APC 102; BT series 91; Cavalier 91; Centaur 91; Centurion 29, 50, 58-9, 159, 191-2; Challenger A30 13, 101; Challenger 1 50, 51; Char B 100, 105, 156; Chieftain 30, 50, 51; Churchill 73, 78, 99, 140, 196; Comet 73, 159; Cromwell 34, 73, 91, 159; Cruiser Mk III 91, 145; Crusader 91, 105, 159; Dragon artillery tractor 58; Grant 66, 156-7; Hornet (Medium C) 202; HMLS Centipede 6; King Tiger 185-6; KV-1 55; Lee 156; Light Tank Mk VIB 45; 'Little Willie' 40-1, 57, 109, 205; 'Male' 15, 33; Matilda I 145, 156; Matilda II 95, 105, 145; Mk I9, 41, 56-7, 61, 109, 120-1, 127, 205; Mk IV 33, 124, 175, 196; Mk IV Replica 87; Mk V 99, 110-1, 174, 202-3; Mk XI 99; Maus 54; Medium B 202; Medium D 203; Medium tank 58, 65; 'Mother' 6, 41, 57, 109, 205; M2 156; 3 Medium tank 98, 105; M4 Sherman 104-5, 140, 156; M4A2 Sherman 68, 122-3; M4A4 Sherman 92, 99; M7 Priest SP gun 99; M10 13; Olifant 191; Panther 162, 191, 199; Panzer III 199; Panzerbefehlswagen 154-5; Ram Kangaroo 98-9; Renault FT 13; Rolls-Royce Armoured Car 62-3; Scorpion Light Tank 74; 7TP 194; Sexton SP gun 99; Sherman Crab 77; Sherman Firefly 13, 92; Sherman V 92-3; Shir 1		Western Front	63, 119, 127, 133
		Weymouth Bay	45
		Wheeled Vehicles Experimental Establishment (WVEE)	87
		Whitehall Pattern Room	74
		Whittenbury, Lt Harold	111
		Wilhelm, Crown Prince	41
		Wilhelm, Kaiser	41
		Wilson, Walter Gordon	41, 100
		Winter Tank Suit	77
		Wireless Set No 19	200-1
		Woolnough, Donald	172-3
		Woolwich Arsenal	6, 87
		Worgret Heath, Dorset	111
		Wright, Bill	49
		Yom Kippur War 1973	193
		Zbrojovka Brno factory	73
		Zeiss, Karl	55
		Zimmerit	199
		Zip suit	77
		Zoot suit	77